KT-514-568

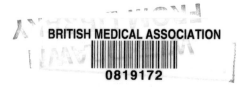

Educational Evaluations
of Children With Special Needs

Educational Evaluations of Children With Special Needs

CLINICAL AND FORENSIC CONSIDERATIONS

David Breiger

Kristen Bishop

G. Andrew H. Benjamin

AMERICAN PSYCHOLOGICAL ASSOCIATION

WASHINGTON, DC

Published by
American Psychological Association
750 First Street, NE
Washington, DC 20002
www.apa.org

To order
APA Order Department
P.O. Box 92984
Washington, DC 20090-2984
Tel: (800) 374-2721; Direct: (202) 336-5510
Fax: (202) 336-5502; TDD/TTY: (202) 336-6123
Online: www.apa.org/pubs/books
E-mail: order@apa.org

In the U.K., Europe, Africa, and the Middle East, copies may be ordered from
American Psychological Association
3 Henrietta Street
Covent Garden, London
WC2E 8LU England

Typeset in Minion by Circle Graphics, Inc., Columbia, MD

Printer: Maple Vail Press, York, PA
Cover Designer: Berg Design, Albany, NY

The opinions and statements published are the responsibility of the authors, and such opinions and statements do not necessarily represent the policies of the American Psychological Association.

Library of Congress Cataloging-in-Publication Data

Breiger, David.
  Educational evaluations of children with special needs : clinical and forensic considerations/ David Breiger, Kristen Bishop, and G. Andrew H. Benjamin.
    pages cm
  Includes bibliographical references and index.
  ISBN-13: 978-1-4338-1575-1
  ISBN-10: 1-4338-1575-3
  1. Learning disabilities—Diagnosis—United States. 2. Children with disabilities—Education—Law and legislation—United States. I. Bishop, Kristen. II. Benjamin, G. Andrew H. III. Title.
  RJ496.L4B74 2013
  618.92'85889—dc23

                                 2013027825

British Library Cataloguing-in-Publication Data
A CIP record is available from the British Library.

Printed in the United States of America
First Edition

http://dx.doi.org/10.1037/14318-000

Forensic Practice in Psychology Series

Bruce D. Sales, PhD, JD, *Series Editor-in-Chief*
G. Andrew H. Benjamin, JD, PhD, ABPP, and Susan R. Hall, JD, PhD, *Associate Series Editors*

Principles of Forensic Report Writing
    Michael Karson and Lavita Nadkarni
Educational Evaluations of Children With Special Needs: Clinical and Forensic Considerations
    David Breiger, Kristen Bishop, and G. Andrew H. Benjamin

Contents

Introduction   3

1. Context and History of Special Education Evaluations   7

2. Law, Ethics, and Competence   21

3. Referral, Clinical Interview, and Psychological Assessment   39

4. Concluding Evaluation and Feedback   63

5. Final Report   75

6. Presentation in Due Process Hearings
    and Postruling Interactions   83

Afterword   93

Appendix A.   Sample Independent Educational
              Evaluation Report   95
Appendix B.   Independent Educational Evaluation:
              Parents' Agreement   115
Appendix C.   Summary of Independent Educational Evaluation
              for Parents   119
Appendix D.   Common Mistakes to Avoid While Conducting
              Independent Educational Evaluations   123

CONTENTS

References   127
Index   133
About the Authors   141

Educational Evaluations
of Children With Special Needs

Introduction

Millions of children receive special education services each year through the public schools. Each one of these children required an evaluation to determine his or her eligibility for services. Although school district personnel conduct the majority of these evaluations, many obtain input from psychologists[1] outside of the school districts.

Psychologists who work with children and adolescents are often the first ones to identify children who may qualify for special education. Psychologists outside of the school district frequently provide information regarding diagnosis and recommendations to help develop an appropriate educational program; however, many of them lack the requisite knowledge of the special education qualification process that will allow them to provide useful assessments and avoid misunderstandings at best and complaints at worst.

---

[1]For purposes of this book, we use the words *psychologist* and *evaluator* interchangeably.

http://dx.doi.org/10.1037/14318-001
Educational Evaluations of Children With Special Needs: Clinical and Forensic Considerations, by D. Breiger, K. Bishop, and G. A. H. Benjamin

PURPOSE OF THE BOOK

This book describes a structured and standardized approach to conducting evaluations of children, specifically to aid in the determination of eligibility for special education services or accommodations in the public school setting. Special attention is paid to independent educational evaluations and situations that may involve considerable tension between families and schools. Both the scholarly literature and the laws that address how a standardized evaluation approach can be conducted are addressed. The chapters provide practical information as well as relevant background material necessary to understand the special education assessment context; this information will assist both psychologists new to and experienced with this area of practice. As a reference, the book facilitates the development of a protocol that guides the evaluation process and minimizes problems with parents or school personnel. As an instructional text, it offers to graduate students and novice psychologists the tools needed to complete educational evaluations.

Psychologists become involved in educational evaluations for children with special needs in a number of ways. Parents contact them directly; psychologists, physicians, and other health care professionals make a referral; school districts request an evaluation; and attorneys may contact them directly or advise parents to contact a psychologist. In each of these cases, the relationship the psychologist has with the child and their family differs; this relationship needs to be clarified at the outset. Such clarification of the psychologist's role is very important to minimize misunderstandings when a family, attorney, or school district requests an evaluation to help determine a child's eligibility for special education. In this book, we provide a detailed model that ensures all parties are aware of the psychologist's role in the evaluation and supports the evaluator's objectivity and ability to conduct a comprehensive assessment.

Children spend much of their waking hours in school settings throughout their childhood. This time in a child's life is critical for the development of academic, cognitive, and social skills. Considerable attention is focused on the quality of the educational experience in public schools; this is an ongoing topic of discussion among educators, politicians, and especially parents. Parents want their children to flourish in positive educational settings, both from an academic perspective as well as a social one. Parents of children with known or suspected special needs (e.g., learning disorders, developmental disabilities, behavioral disorders, medical disorders) have heightened concerns regarding their child's experience in and out of school.

Many psychologists who have a background in child development and assessment are familiar with disorders that occur in childhood are challenged by participating in evaluations for special education, especially when there is significant discord between parents and school districts or if the case might involve testifying at an administrative hearing. The process that we describe in the book will help psychologists implement an assessment format that will prepare them to effectively deal with difficult cases or those that may end up going to a hearing. School psychologists may also benefit from seeing how the process unfolds from outside of the confines of the school, and they may learn to better identify independent psychologists who use a best-practices approach. Finally, parents may gain a better understanding of the context of evaluations for special education qualification and use the information to help inform their choice of an evaluator.

Because of the high-stakes nature of qualification for special education services and the confusing process (McBride, Dumont, & Willis, 2011), the potential for significant conflict between families and schools is great. Often difficulties arise in the evaluation process because of miscommunications and misunderstanding on the part of parents regarding the process of identification of students who are eligible for support or specially designed instruction. Federal and state laws that govern this process are often perplexing, and unfortunately this often leads to confusion not only for parents but also for psychologists, some of whom may not be familiar with the process. Disagreements can even result in legal proceedings that may involve psychologists in a forensic environment that many find unfamiliar and uncomfortable. In this book, we provide information to decrease the possibility that a psychologist will be involved in a due process hearing, but we also provide information to help psychologists prepare themselves if a hearing is necessary.

There are many books on child assessment that emphasize theory, test development, and the characteristics and interpretation of tests. We do not cover the diagnostic features of disorders that occur in childhood or discuss the best instruments for making diagnoses, because this information can be found in other texts; instead, we outline the actual process of conducting an assessment, relying on our clinical experience and borrowing from a successful model developed for family evaluation in custody litigation (Benjamin & Gollan, 2003).

Organization

The chapters of this book cover three overarching categories. In Chapters 1 and 2, we describe the preparatory work that one should accomplish before conducting evaluations. We briefly discuss the context of special education services, the laws that govern provisions of services, and differences between evaluations conducted by school districts and those by independent psychologists.

In Chapters 3 through 6, we focus on the assessment procedures in conducting educational evaluations of children with special needs. We discuss the preevaluation procedures, which avoid both the appearance of conflict of interest and perceived bias by evaluator. We also discuss the parameters of confidentiality and fee agreements. We then outline the phases of the evaluation, offering practical suggestions that lead to efficient, thorough, and transparent collection of data. The structure of the interview with the parents, school districts, teachers, and psychological assessment are explained. Following this, we discuss providing feedback to families and school districts, report writing, and presentations in administrative hearings.

Appendix A contains a sample report so that readers can get an idea of the scope of a comprehensive evaluation. The case material is discussed in each section to illustrate how the approach is applied at each step of the evaluation process.

Context and History of
Special Education Evaluations

A large population of children in the U.S. public school system are receiving special education services. A 2011 report by the National Center for Education Statistics revealed that in the 2008–2009 school year 6.5 million children, representing 13% of the public school population, received special education services (Aud et al., 2011). These services were provided for children deemed eligible under the Individuals With Disabilities Education Improvement Act of 2004 (IDEIA). Although this report showed a slight decrease in the percentage of children receiving special education services overall in recent years, the last 30 years have seen a significant increase in the number of public school children receiving special education services. For instance, in the 1980–1981 school year, only 10.1% of public school children received special education services.

http://dx.doi.org/10.1037/14318-002
Educational Evaluations of Children With Special Needs: Clinical and Forensic Considerations, by D. Breiger,
K. Bishop, and G. A. H. Benjamin

Children can qualify for special education services because of one or more mental, physical, and emotional conditions that affect their ability to learn. It is unclear how many children could qualify for a formal diagnosis in the *Diagnostic and Statistical Manual of Mental Disorders* (*DSM–IV*; American Psychiatric Association, 1994) because only a limited number of large-scale studies have addressed this topic. However, the Methodology for Epidemiology of Mental Disorders in Children and Adolescents study revealed some significant prevalence rates for children ages 9 through 17 (Shaffer et al., 1996). The findings indicated that nearly 21% of all children have a diagnosable mental illness based on *DSM–III–R* (American Psychiatric Association, 1987) criteria.[1]

More recently, a prevalence rate of 17.1% was found for children ages 11 through 17, with anxiety disorders (6.9%) and disruptive disorders (6.4%) being the most prevalent *DSM–IV* diagnoses (Roberts, Roberts, & Xing, 2007). The researchers further narrowed this population to 11.1% of children with at least moderate impairment resulting from their diagnosis (Roberts et al., 2007). Similarly, another study revealed a 13.1% prevalence rate for *DSM–IV* diagnoses among children ages 8 through 15 (Merikangas et al., 2010). These large-scale studies often included anxiety disorders, attention-deficit/hyperactivity disorder (ADHD), conduct disorder, mood disorders, eating disorders, and substance use disorders (Merikangas et al., 2010; Roberts et al., 2007; Shaffer et al., 1996).

Conditions such as pervasive developmental disorders (PDDs), including autism spectrum disorders (ASDs), a category that includes Asperger's disorder, are typically not included in these prevalence rates, and yet the prevalence rates of PDDs are growing. Not including PDDs in the prevalence rates results in a serious underestimation of the overall impact on school districts across the nation given the growing number of children

---

[1] This book references past editions of the *DSM*; a new edition (*DSM–5*) was published in 2013, after this book went to press. The World Health Organization has also developed the *International Statistical Classification of Diseases and Related Health Problems* (*ICD-10*; World Health Organization, 2010). The *ICD-10* provides a rich diagnostic framework that integrates social, psychological, biological, and cultural contributors (American Psychological Association, 2005; American Psychological Association, Council of Representatives, 2008). Given these changes, and the shift under the Patient Protection and Affordable Care Act of 2010 toward *ICD-10* functional diagnoses, we recommend that *ICD-10* be used for diagnoses of children who could qualify for special educational services.

being diagnosed and in need of special education services. One study that reviewed previous epidemiological research found an approximate ASD prevalence rate of 0.6%, or one in 167 children (Fombonne, 2005). The Autism and Developmental Disabilities Monitoring Network (http://www.cdc.gov/ncbddd/autism/addm.html) recently reported a rise in the prevalence rate of ASDs among 8-year-olds across 14 surveillance sites; as of 2006, one in 150 children could be accurately diagnosed with an ASD, compared with the 2008 rate of one in 88 (Centers for Disease Control and Prevention, 2008). This appears to be the highest prevalence rate currently reported. One recent large-scale study reported a 17% increase in children diagnosed with developmental disabilities over a 12-year period (Boyle et al., 2011). These researchers found that 15% of children ages 3 through 17 were reported as having a developmental disability. Furthermore, the authors explained how the increasing numbers of children being diagnosed with ADHD and autism have contributed to this overall trend.

Recent publications suggest that prevalence rates of children with physical, mental, and emotional disabilities are growing, but the opposite is true for special education funding. Although the number of children receiving special education services is rising, the funding allotted for these services is not proportionate (New America Foundation, 2012). In fact, federal education programs, including those that provide special education, are facing significant cutbacks that have been predicted to set funding back nearly a decade, while the number of special education students continues to rise (National Education Association, 2012). Accurate and easily accessible documentation of state and district special education spending is unavailable, which presents a challenge in determining spending trends (Scull & Winkler, 2011). However, scholars have estimated that the 13% of special education students accounted for 21% of educational spending (Scull & Winkler, 2011). Given projected cutbacks, this population is at risk of losing invaluable educational services, making quality evaluations and recommendations even more critical.

These rising prevalence rates and diminution of funding for services present a challenge for families, educators, and evaluators alike. There is a rapidly increasing need for educational services, and many parents are look-ing for strategies for how best to advocate for their child so that the child can receive timely and appropriate services (such an advocacy resource is available for parents if they obtain the TeamChild, 2008, education advo-cacy manual). Well-trained psychologists can provide consultation and efficacious services for children and families that will help them achieve favorable outcomes contemplated by IDEIA's findings (20 U.S.C. §1400(c) (5-14)). Psychologists trained in the treatment of multicultural popula-tions are particularly needed to consult with and help train school district personnel (for more information, see the American Psychological Associa-tion's *Guidelines on Multicultural Education, Training, Research, Practice, and Organizational Change for Psychologists,* http://www.apa.org/pi/oema/ resources/policy/multicultural-guidelines.aspx). The National Association of School Psychologists is aware of this problem and has identified recruit-ment of a more diverse population of school psychologists as one of its strategic goals (National Association of School Psychologists, 2009).

THE LEGAL STANDARDS

Federal laws have fundamentally changed how the unique needs of U.S. children are served. Under both IDEIA and Section 504 of the Rehabilita-tion Act of 1973, free appropriate public education must be provided by the states and their school districts to meet students' individual needs. Ernst, Pelletier, and Simpson (2008) correctly noted that a child with a simple diagnosis would not necessarily be eligible for services under either law.

Section 504 provides services and accommodations if the child has a physical or mental impairment that substantially limits a major life activ-ity (Definitions, 34 C.F.R. § 104.3(j) (2010)), which includes

- learning,
- walking,
- seeing,
- hearing,
- speaking,
- breathing,

- caring for oneself, and
- performing manual tasks.

Although Section 504 has a more expansive definition of *disability* than IDEIA, an individual's rights under IDEIA are more clearly defined. Under IDEIA, children who fall within one or more of the following categories of disability, if found eligible for special education services, must receive special education and related services to promote academic progress (20 U.S.C. § 1401(3)):

- mental retardation (now referred to as *intellectual disability*),
- hearing impairments (including deafness and deafness–blindness),
- speech or language impairments,
- visual impairments (including blindness),
- serious emotional disturbance,
- orthopedic impairments,
- autism,
- traumatic brain injury,
- developmental delay,
- multiple disabilities,
- other health impairments, and/or
- specific learning disabilities.

States and their school district have an affirmative duty to identify all students residing within the districts who might need special education services. Under the law, this duty is called *child find,* and each district is required to develop procedures to ensure that each student is identified and evaluated (IDEIA, 20 U.S.C. § 1412(a)(3)).

TYPES OF EVALUATION

Families may seek an evaluation for their child through a number of different methods or channels. Often, after learning that their child is struggling academically or behaviorally, parents speak with an educator or school counselor to find out how to proceed. It also is common for parents to bring up their concerns during a routine appointment with the child's pediatrician or family doctor. When this occurs, the doctor may refer the family to a local psychologist to determine whether an evaluation is needed. The physician may also tell the family to seek assistance from the school first or to simultaneously access both a psychologist and the school's process.

In some cases, parents seek evaluation only from the child's pediatrician or a child psychiatrist, and not the school—for example, a parent who suspects that the child has ADHD and wishes for the child to receive a diagnosis only for the purpose of receiving treatment through medication. Many parents are concerned about labeling their children and may choose to not inform schools of diagnostic and treatment decisions. In these cases, the family may or may not choose to consult a psychologist and may not inform the school until some treatment is received.

Other families will independently seek assistance from a psychologist in their area, rather than talking with a health care provider; for example, they may simply call a psychologist and ask for an appointment to discuss some concerns they have about their child. Therefore, the child would be evaluated and a report provided to the family with little interaction between the evaluator and school. In this event, the resulting evaluation report may come as a surprise to school professionals, not contain important information that a teacher or district could have provided, fail to fit well with the school district's process, and result in an adversarial process. Families have a right to request an *independent educational evaluation* (IEE) if the school district fails to determine whether the student has a disability, how the disability affects a student's progress in school, and what services would likely address the student's individual needs. If the parents believe that the results of the school district's evaluation do not address their concerns, they may obtain an IEE outside of the school environment (Independent Educational Evaluation, 34 C.F.R. § 300.502(a)(3)(i) (2010)).

PURPOSE, QUALIFICATION, AND IMPORTANCE OF SPECIAL EDUCATION SERVICES

Evaluations of children to determine whether special education services are needed can be initiated by either the child's parent or a state or local educational agency, as outlined in Section 504 of the Rehabilitation Act of 1973

(Nondiscrimination on the Basis of Handicap, 34 C.F.R. § 104 (2010)) and IDEIA (20 U.S.C. § 1400). The initial evaluations are conducted for the purpose of determining whether the child has a disability and, if he or she does, the child's educational needs. The content of these evaluations is governed by Section 504 or IDEIA and state requirements (in Chapter 2 of this volume, we provide a detailed review about how the laws work).

Beyond determining eligibility, one of the goals of the school district's evaluation, and perhaps an IEE evaluation, is to gain information about a child's academic functioning for later use in the creation of an *individualized education plan* (IEP), or Section 504 plan. It is the IEP that ultimately guides the special education services a child receives. This plan describes the accommodations and modifications that are appropriate for the student. The IEP team consists of individuals such as the parents, general education teacher, special education teacher, school psychologist, principal, the child (when appropriate), and "other individuals who have knowledge or special expertise regarding the child, including related services personnel as appropriate" (IDEIA, 2004; IEP Team, 34 C.F.R. § 300.321(a)(6) (2010)). In constructing the IEP, this team considers

  (i) the strengths of the child;
  (ii) the concerns of the parents for enhancing the education of
      their child;
  (iii) the results of the initial or most recent evaluation of the child; and
  (iv) the academic, developmental, and functional needs of the child.
      (IDEIA, 2004; Development, Review, and Revision, 34 C.F.R.
      § 300.324(a)(i)–(iv) (2010))

Different rights and services are delivered under Section 504 as opposed to IDEIA. Whereas Section 504 provides broader protections for any individual with a disability and access to accommodations, IDEIA outlines very specific eligibility criteria and special education services. A child with a disability can be afforded protection under Section 504 and receive services governed by IDEIA, but it is possible for a child to receive protection and accommodations under Section 504 while not being eligible for special education services under IDEIA.

CLINICAL VERSUS EDUCATIONAL FRAMEWORK

Although both independent clinical psychologists and school psychologists strive to determine how and why a child is struggling academically, they are likely to approach this differently given their respective backgrounds and duties. Understanding these differences can provide insight for those conducting assessments and assist clinical psychologists as they navigate the educational environment. Both independent clinical psychologists and school psychologists have obtained clinical education, training, and experience, and both have ethical obligations to conduct objective, comprehensive evaluations. Independent clinical psychologists and school psychologists both practice within a specific setting, population, and culture. School psychologists may be more familiar with the challenges of the particular school environment, how the laws that govern or mandate a child receiving special education services are interpreted and relied on within that school environment, and the day-to-day culture of the school and the norms of the classroom. School psychologists have different constraints placed on their activities (e.g., time, role, measurement tools) than independent clinical psychologists. The latter may have more experience and training with different clinical populations (e.g., medical disorders, psychiatric disorders, psychological treatments, research) than school psychologists.

The different perspectives or frameworks that guide evaluators influence both their purpose and approach to evaluation. An independent clinical psychologist will conduct an evaluation to formulate a diagnosis and obtain information about a child's patterns of strengths and weaknesses as well as information regarding his or her social-emotional functioning. Information regarding family functioning also is gathered. Finally, the clinical psychologist will interpret the information in the context of the child's medical, developmental, social, and cultural histories. The evaluation conducted by the school psychologist usually will be more focused on the goal of determining the child's eligibility for special education services (Kanne, Randolph, & Farmer, 2008). Both professionals strive to determine how and why the child is struggling, offer their diagnosis, identify what services would be most beneficial, and make recommendations accordingly. However, many independent evaluators are likely to face challenges working within a particular school setting.

These challenges can lead school-based professionals to question the validity and reliability of an independent evaluator's clinical data and recommendations. Interprofessional barriers include a lack of collaboration across professions, perceived role differences, differences in the approach and purpose of recommendations, profession-based language differences, and discrepancies between the professions' governing laws or policies (Cleary & Scott, 2011; Ernst et al., 2008; Kanne et al., 2008). Awareness of these differences and how they can lead to reports and recommendations being viewed as lacking validity is central to creating solid recommendations.

One such difference is the tendency for non–school-based evaluators to approach assessment and diagnosis with the most recent edition of the *DSM* in mind, whereas school-based evaluators are guided by Section 504 and IDEIA (e.g., evidence of educational impairment). For this reason, when school officials receive an evaluation report structured only around the *DSM*, they may see it as insufficient or incomplete for the school setting. One study that reviewed the assessment practices and eligibility determinations in court cases surrounding children with ASDs (Fogt, Miller, & Zirkel, 2003) found that whereas only 54% of the cases cited the *DSM* when considering special education eligibility, 80% of the cases cited IDEIA or other state regulations. Furthermore, the researchers noted that IDEIA, not the *DSM*, was considered the authority for determining eligibility and suggested that evaluators incorporate these eligibility criteria within all school evaluations (Fogt et al., 2003).

Given the importance of IDEIA in the educational setting, the credibility of an evaluator's diagnosis and recommendations will be strengthened by the psychological evidence collected and organized to meet the elements of the law during the assessment process and in the resulting reports. In fact, it is seen as not only beneficial but necessary. Put simply, some argue that "while the *DSM–IV* criteria are professionally helpful, they are neither legally required nor sufficient for determining educational placement" (Wilkinson, 2010, pp. 129–130). When conducting an evaluation to be reviewed and integrated into a school context, it is best to discuss the evaluation evidence under the framework of the laws and mandates of that context.

Considering and grounding the assessment process in education-related laws such as IDEIA will likely increase the transferability and meaningfulness of the evaluators' recommendations. In turn, school professionals will need to spend less time translating the report and recommendations into the educational framework needed to determine special education eligibility.

Another challenge independent evaluators may face is the disclosure of personal information by the child or family members. It is common for parents to reveal information about themselves, a spouse or partner, caregiver, or other family member during the clinical intake or assessment process. This information could include details regarding the quality of the parents' relationship, parenting difficulties, current or past abuse of the child, challenges with other siblings or family members, drug and/or alcohol abuse by a family member, and other personal details. When an evaluation is conducted in a setting outside the school environment, individuals may feel even more comfortable revealing this personal information. An extensive disclosure and informed-consent process is critical in order to maintain the respect and dignity of the children's families. Such a process will prevent parents from being surprised and make them less inclined to feel betrayed, feeling states that often drive dissatisfaction with psychological services.

Personal information about a family that is revealed may complicate the evaluator's assessment process. For example, if a child is receiving an evaluation because he or she is struggling in school with inattention, incomplete schoolwork, and impulse control problems during class, the evaluator may conduct the assessment with a hypothesis of ADHD in mind. However, if the evaluation evidence suggests that extensive conflict in the home has recently occurred and the parents are discussing divorce, this may shed a different light on the child's behavior. A child may qualify for special education services if he or she has been diagnosed with a condition that is contributing to his or her academic challenges, but not if family conflict and the ensuing stress on the child are responsible for the symptoms. Long-standing patterns of behavior will assist the clinician in determining the etiology of the difficulties. It may be that a combination of a diagnosable condition and a situational stressor exists. If this is the case, and the evaluator determines that the child meets the criteria for a diagnosis, the evaluator must delineate the interplay between the stressors at home and the child's school performance. Presenting a family with a report that outlines the child's psychological functioning and environmental stressors that may be exacerbating symptoms can be challenging and place the evaluator in an uncomfortable situation, but, as we discuss later in this book, such a meeting is strongly recommended.

TYPES OF TESTING

The No Child Left Behind Act of 2001 (NCLB; 2002) is an amendment of the original Elementary and Secondary Education Act of 1965. The purpose of NCLB "is to ensure that all children have a fair, equal, and significant opportunity to obtain a high-quality education and reach, at a minimum, proficiency on challenging State academic achievement standards and state academic assessments" (20 U.S.C. § 6301). Note that all children are included and that this amendment of the original 1965 law applies to children with disabilities. One of the primary purposes of NCLB is the increased accountability of schools and states for student achievement.

To ensure this accountability, and that appropriate academic standards are met, high-stakes testing is often used (Nichols, 2007). *High-stakes testing* in the educational setting is commonly thought of as testing used to make decisions such as whether a student can graduate high school or move to the next grade level (American Psychological Association, 2012). The outcomes of high-stakes and large-scale testing can carry significant consequences for the student, the school district, or both (Ysseldyke et al., 2004). Given the potential consequences of a poor performance on a high-stakes test, it is important that students with disabilities receive appropriate accommodations.

Students with disabilities are required, under both IDEIA and NCLB, to participate in high-stakes testing (Lai & Berkeley, 2012; Luke & Schwartz, 2007). Although significant questions about the validity of high-stakes testing in improving teaching and student achievement exist (Nichols, 2007; Supovitz, 2009), it is likely to continue being used in order to ensure school and student accountability. Therefore, determining how best to support students with disabilities during these tests is crucial.

For children with disabilities, an important result of an evaluation is likely to be the determination of accommodations that can be implemented in the classroom and during testing. These accommodations can provide scaffolding or support in areas in which the student struggles because of a disability. Common types of accommodations provided relate to timing (e.g., extended time, frequent breaks), responses (e.g., typing, responding verbally), the setting (individual or small group, reduced stimuli), presentation (print type or size), and equipment/materials (writing or reading aids; Lai & Berkeley, 2012; Luke & Schwartz, 2007).

Depending on the state and school district, the degree to which students receive accommodations varies significantly (Lai & Berkeley, 2012). Therefore, it is important that the evaluator be aware of both the state's and school district's approach to accommodations, especially while constructing the recommendations. In addition, evaluators need to be aware of the research that supports particular accommodations for children with specific disabilities to ensure that the accommodation is likely to have the intended benefits and be accepted within the educational setting (Lai & Berkeley, 2012).

CONCLUSION

A large number of students are currently receiving special education services or are eligible to receive special education services or accommodations. The process for evaluation and qualification for special education services is often difficult for families to understand and can lead to confusion and sometimes conflict between schools and families. Psychologists outside of the school are often involved in evaluating children and making recommendations regarding educational plans. It is important that psychologists conducting these evaluations are familiar with the laws governing special education and accommodations as well as the school environment. This will enhance their ability to develop collaborative relationships with everyone working to help the child succeed in school.

2

Law, Ethics, and Competence

All children ages 3 to 21 who have a mental, physical, or emotional impairment that affects the ability to learn are entitled to additional support and services to help them access a meaningful education. The federally funded Early Intervention Program (Part C of the Individuals With Disabilities Education Improvement Act of 2004) also provides special education services for children younger than 3 years. The legal rights of children with disabilities include evaluation, an appropriate educational program, and due process protections. Both federal and state laws protect the educational rights of students with disabilities. Although state laws differ among the 50 jurisdictions, and the different districts within each jurisdiction may interpret and implement the laws somewhat differently (Lai & Berkeley, 2012; MacFarlane & Kanaya, 2009), the federal laws

http://dx.doi.org/10.1037/14318-003
Educational Evaluations of Children With Special Needs: Clinical and Forensic Considerations, by D. Breiger, K. Bishop, and G. A. H. Benjamin

have raised standards across the jurisdictions. Nevertheless, differences do exist:

> By examining the legal code, we found wide variability in eligibility criteria between the states. It is important to recognize that this variability has the largest impact on children who are clinically diagnosed with [an autism-spectrum disorder] (e.g., Asperger's disorder). An ASD child would qualify for Autism services in a state that includes ASDs in their eligibility but may fail to do so in a state that requires a clinical diagnosis of Autism. In these latter cases, children with ASDs will likely be placed into "Other Health Impairment" or "Emotional Disturbance." (MacFarlane & Kanaya, 2009, p. 667)

Psychologists who work in this arena should obtain the written standards and procedures of the school district and the department of education in the state or territory where they will practice (for a directory of the state and territory education agencies, see http://wdcrobcolp01.ed.gov/programs/erod/org_list.cfm?category_ID=SEA).

Significant differences exist among legal, psychological, and educational professionals in the ways they approach data collection and the synthesis of information in the educational context. Legal professionals must frame their work within the pertinent judicial and legal standards. Psychologists gather information from semistructured clinical interviews, psychological testing, self-report measurement, third party collateral reports, and relevant records. These data are transformed into a cohesive summary that guides recommendations about how to promote child adjustment. Educational professionals depend more on functional and academic information about the child, including that culled from in-class assessments (often called *curriculum-based measures*) that are completed by the general education teacher.

These differences translate into important practical considerations for psychologists conducting educational evaluations. Application of scientific values (e.g., arriving at a conclusion only after multiple-measure corroboration) in psychological assessment is one of the highest priorities in evaluations, yet it is important to ensure that the information gathered for these assessments is obtained within the constraints of the legal

LAW, ETHICS, AND COMPETENCE

rules and will have practical usefulness within the educational context: "Recommendations are much more likely to be integrated into the [individualized education plan] when they address needs specific to the school environment" (Ernst, Pelletier, & Simpson, 2008, p. 968). Access to and use of data must both meet the ethical standards for psychologists as well as the constraints of legal rules. It is critical that psychologists incorporate into their assessment process an understanding of the prevailing legal standards (e.g., obtaining the local school district and state standards and procedures that flesh out the federal law; American Psychological Association, 2002, 2010). The more psychologists use the terms of the substantive law to organize their recitation of the evaluation's findings, the more likely it is that legal and educational professionals will find the discussion of psychological reports useful. Indeed, psychology's ethical guidelines call for the exercise of such knowledge: "When assuming forensic roles, psychologists are or become reasonably familiar with the judicial or administrative rules governing their roles" (American Psychological Association, 2010, Standard 2.01f; http://www.apa.org/ethics/code/index. aspx?item=5).

To facilitate an understanding of the primary legal and scientific considerations in conducting evaluations, in this chapter we highlight both the legally crafted standards used in educational cases and the scientific considerations in conducting evaluations in school settings.

EVALUATION FOR SERVICES UNDER THE EDUCATION LAWS

As discussed in Chapter 1 of this volume, Section 504 of the Rehabilitation Act of 1973 (Nondiscrimination on the Basis of Handicap, 34 C.F.R. § 104 (2010)) and IDEIA have created the legal framework that prevents states from allowing school districts to exclude children with disabilities.

Requests for evaluations (a referral for a special education evaluation used to be called a *focus of concern*) typically are made by parents. School districts will expect a written referral, and no action will occur unless such a referral is made. District policy will also specify whether the referral goes to the school principal or a specific district representative.

Requests should urge that the school evaluate the child in all areas related to the specific concerns about the child under both Section 504 and IDEIA, because the child may not be eligible for special education under the more narrow standards of IDEIA. Psychologists can assist parents in formulating a sufficient request by urging them to submit supporting records from the health care providers who have evaluated or treated the child, delineate concrete examples based on their own observations about the specific concerns, and integrate the corroborating evidence from the health care records and observations about the specific concerns in their request.

The school district should confirm that the request for evaluation was received and provide written notification of the decision about whether the child's concerns will be evaluated after a review of the school's records and the parents' request occurs. Although no evaluation timelines are established in Section 504, IDEIA specifies that once the parents provide consent, an initial evaluation to determine whether the child has a disability shall be conducted within 60 days (20 U.S.C. § 1414(a)(1)(C)(i)(I)). State laws typically will establish a timeline for notification and content of the notification.

Legal Process if the School Agrees to Evaluate or Decides to Pursue an Evaluation

Before the district conducts any evaluation of the child, the parents must consent. The district may pursue a hearing if the parents refuse to provide consent (20 U.S.C. § 1414(a)(1)(D)(ii)). Once consent has been obtained to evaluate the child for special education eligibility, an initial evaluation is conducted to determine whether the child has a disability (20 U.S.C. § 1414(a)(1)(C)(i)(I)). State laws typically specify the time frame within which the district must complete the evaluation and determine whether the child needs special education services. It is possible for the district and parents to decide on another timeline, although such a decision should be documented.

Under the law, assessment in all areas of suspected disability must occur. If the district has stopped the evaluation once a student is found eligible for special education in a particular area, and has not addressed the other concerns raised by the parents, the parents have the right to insist on a comprehensive evaluation in all areas of concern (20 U.S.C. § 1414(b)(3)(B)).

Relevant functional, developmental, and academic data about the student must be collected using a variety of assessment approaches (20 U.S.C. § 1414(b)(2)(A)). Evaluation tests cannot discriminate on the basis of race, culture, or gender; any testing must be conducted in the student's native language or other mode of communication, such as American Sign Language (20 U.S.C. § 1414(b)(3)(A)). Although district staff will conduct most of the assessment, they must seek external expertise if particular assessment skills are outside of the scope of their training. This is often the point at which psychologists become involved in the process. If the district seeks further clarification by engaging outside expertise, it is their responsibility to fund the evaluation. Sometimes the district may ask a family to use its insurance benefits or other sources of funding, but if the family refuses, the district must pay for any outside evaluations.

An eligibility-determination group will focus on the evaluation to determine whether the student has a disability and if so, how the disability affects the student's progress in school and what services would likely address his or her individual needs. Before such a team meeting, the parents may request the evaluation results. That way, if the results do not address the parents' concerns, they will be better prepared to insist on an independent educational evaluation (IEE) and have such a request granted if other, contradictory data suggest that the school district's evaluation is insufficient. The parents should seek outside consultation from a psychologist to help them organize the contradictory data into a compelling narrative. Note that the law does not preclude the parents' consultant from interacting with the appropriate school personnel before and during the eligibility-determination group's meeting.

School districts must identify one person in each district to coordinate their efforts to comply with Section 504. Under the law, each district must identify the procedures and the name of the person designated as a Section 504 compliance officer (Designation of Responsible Employee, 34 C.F.R. § 104.7 (2010)). Before the eligibility-determination group meets, parents should request that the district's Section 504 program representative participate as part of the group. If the student is deemed to not be eligible for special education under IDEIA, services may still be provided under Section 504. In most states, parents must be given notice of the meeting; they have the right to attend it, and parents should request to be a part of the eligibility-determination team. However, recent research findings suggest that the procedures for implementing Section 504 differ markedly from district to district:

> There is a disturbing inconsistency related to how students are determined to be eligible under Section 504 . . . only 54% of the respondents indicated that a disability must be diagnosed for a student to be eligible to receive Section 504 services. Likewise, only 61% indicated that a significant impairment to a major life function must be established for a student to be eligible to receive Section 504 services. (Madaus & Shaw, 2007, p. 374)

Parents will be provided a copy of the evaluation report and documentation about the district's decision regarding eligibility.

Most states' laws include a time frame within which the eligibility decision for special education must be announced and another time frame within which an individualized education program (IEP) is designed. A specialized team crafts the IEP, which details the instruction and services a student with disabilities should receive. The IEP team usually is made up of the following people (20 U.S.C. § 1414(d)(1)(B)):

- parent or guardian;
- at least one of the child's general education teachers;
- at least one of the child's special education teachers or, where appropriate, special education provider;
- a district representative, such as a director of special education;
- an individual who can interpret the evaluation data;
- the child (if appropriate); and
- transition service providers (e.g., vocational specialists or someone from an outside agency, such as a representative from the state's Office of Developmental Disabilities).

The team is not limited to the people in this list. IDEIA specifically allows others who "have knowledge or special expertise regarding the child" to participate on the IEP team. The team certainly could include a consulting psychologist hired by the parents. Both the district and the parent have the right to decide who has the expertise regarding the child and to suggest who else should serve on the team. Most states require that the district notify the parents of the purpose of the IEP meeting, its time and location, and who will be attending. If necessary, meetings can occur by telephone or videoconference (20 U.S.C. § 1414(f)).

Sometimes members of the IEP team may have to miss one or more IEP meetings. The parents and the school district may agree in writing to excuse a team member from a meeting, even if the meeting involves a discussion regarding the team member's specialization. The IEP team member who is excused, though, must submit written input about the development of the IEP to the parents and the school district before the meeting (20 U.S.C. §§ 1414(d)(1)(B)–(C)).

The mandatory contents of an IEP should guide the psychologist as to how to arrange the psychological evidence under the concrete categories within the Impressions section of the final report (see Chapter 5, this volume). The IEP must include the following (20 U.S.C. § 1414(d)(1)(A)):

- a statement about the child's current levels of education and functional performance;
- annual educational goals;
- a statement about how the child's progress will be measured and when periodic reports in the child's progress should be provided;
- descriptions of all services a child will receive, both in the general education classroom setting and in a special education setting;
- a description of "related services" the student will receive, such as speech and language therapy, psychotherapy, and so on;
- a description of all program modifications to be provided, such as modified reading materials, a reader for examinations and other assignments, and tape recorder for lectures;

- a determination of whether the child needs assistive technology devices and services (i.e., equipment that enhances or maintains the capabilities of the student, e.g., a computer or custom keyboard);
- a decision about eligibility for adaptive physical education and, if the student is eligible, how this will be provided;
- a description of how the student will participate in general education classes and activities and if not, why;
- any accommodations the student will have for taking state or district achievement tests;
- extended school year services, if determined necessary by the IEP team;
- aversive interventions, if any, required for the student;
- the location, duration, and frequency of the services to be delivered;
- dates on which services will begin; and
- transition services that would begin no later than the IEP.

To be in effect when the student turns 16 (or younger, if determined appropriate by the IEP team), two specific services must be provided to prepare the child for an adult life to promote movement from school to postschool activities, including college, vocational training programs, independent living programs, and supported employment (20 U.S.C. § 1414(d)(1)(A)(i)(VIII)): (a) appropriate measurable postsecondary goals and (b) specific transition services needed to assist the student in reaching those goals.

Before an IEP is implemented, the parents must agree to the services. A school district cannot override the parents' refusal to consent to the initiation of special education services (20 U.S.C. § 1414(a)(1)(D)(ii)). However, if the child is found eligible for special education and an IEP is never implemented because of lack of parental consent, it is possible that services under Section 504 can be provided.

IEPs are supposed to be reviewed annually, but if a review does not occur, that district must continue to follow the existing plan. An IEP meeting can be requested before the annual review to delineate what services identified in the IEP are being delivered, what behaviors of the child have not changed, and how the placement of the child should change. The revised IEP should anticipate a child's changing needs and incorporate new information that has emerged during the provision of services up to that point. A request of any team member, or a change of circumstances, can lead to an IEP team meeting review. Written documentation, without a meeting, can change the child's IEP if the parents and district agree to the changes (20 U.S.C. § 1414(d)(3)(D)).

Comprehensive reevaluations, with testing, of the child must occur once every 3 years (20 U.S.C. § 1414(a)(2)(B)(ii)). If the school district determines that the educational service needs of the child warrant a reevaluation, or if the parent or teacher requests a reevaluation, the comprehensive reevaluation must be done (20 U.S.C. § 1414(a)(2)(A)).

Legal Process if the School Declines to Evaluate the Child or Denies Eligibility

Parents can challenge the district's decision if the school declines to evaluate the child or the child is denied eligibility for special education services. In some instances, the district's evaluation methodology will not reveal subtle neuropsychological conditions that affect learning; some neurocognitive and sensorimotor deficits will avoid identification with the psychoeducational methodology used by school district personnel (Ernst et al., 2008).

Parents can request an IEE at the district's expense by a qualified person who is not an employee of the district (Independent Educational Evaluation, 34 C.F.R. § 300.502(a)(3)(i) (2010)). The parents can request an IEE if concerns arise about the school's decision or the results of the district's evaluation; such a request may be necessary for the district to fully involve the parents in the planning and implementation of services (Schrank, Miller, Caterino, & Desrochers, 2006). Although school districts typically have a list of the evaluators who can perform IEEs (Independent Educational Evaluation, 34 C.F.R. § 300.502(a)(2) (2010)), they can be done by someone who is not on the district's list (Independent Educational Evaluation, 34 C.F.R. § 300.502(a)(3)(i) (2010)). Unless the school district objects to the IEE, the district must pay for it (Independent Educational Evaluation, 34 C.F.R. § 300.502(b)(2) (2010)). At a hearing that must occur without unnecessary delay, if the hearing officer determines that the district's evaluation is appropriate, the family still has a right to an independent evaluation, at the parents' expense (Independent Educational Evaluation, 34 C.F.R § 300.502(b)(3) (2010)). Parents are entitled to one IEE at public expense each time the district conducts an evaluation with which the parents disagree (Independent Educational Evaluation, 34 C.F.R. § 300.502(b)(5) (2010)).

If the district balks at paying for the IEE, the parents, in consultation with their psychologist, should attempt to negotiate with the school district about the IEE parameters. A district will be less likely to force the matter into a hearing if it believes that the parents are acting reasonably. Parents should consider making the following suggestions to the district (Ernst et al., 2008; TeamChild, 2008):

- suggest three independent evaluators with whom the district has worked before and with whom the school district appears to have developed good working relationships;
- identify a cap for the cost of the IEE or agree to split the cost in some way; and
- delineate the specific school district input, in addition to a thorough records review, by identifying in advance the collateral interviews that would occur with the teacher, principal (or his or her representative), and the district evaluation specialist.

If no compromise can be arranged quickly, the district must move forward and either request a hearing or fund the IEE. Evidence of the parents attempting to act reasonably with the district in light of its flat refusal to fund the evaluation will carry some weight with the hearing officer.

DISPUTE RESOLUTION

IEP-related disputes that arise are generally resolved in one of two ways: (a) mediation or (b) administrative proceedings.

Mediation

IDEIA mandates that states provide free mediation services to parents and school districts to resolve conflicts about the child's special education program (20 U.S.C. § 1415(e)(1)). The parents and school district have to agree to participate in this form of dispute resolution. If mediation with a third, neutral party is successful, the parents and school district sign a legally binding agreement that delineates the resolution. The parents and school district are both obligated to carry out the terms of the agreement. However, if a further conflict emerges, the terms in contention can be enforced only by a state or federal court. The written mediation agreement can be used as evidence (20 U.S.C. § 1415(e)(2)(F)).

Administrative Proceedings

At what is referred to as a *due process hearing*, the parents and the school district (the parties in the hearing) each have an opportunity to present evidence and witnesses (20 U.S.C. § 1415(f)). A *hearing officer* or *administrative law judge* (the specific title depends on each state's law) makes a written decision based on the facts and the law, with the party that files the complaint having to prove its case by a preponderance of the evidence (*Schaffer v. Weast*, 2005).

Although the parents are not required to be represented by a lawyer, they would be wise to retain a lawyer who specializes in educational law so that the case is prepared and presented in the most efficacious manner possible. At a minimum, parents should consult with an attorney to establish whether there is a basis for a legal claim against the school district. The hearing officer can award attorneys' fees to the parents if they win the due process hearing. Attorneys' fees also can be awarded to the school district, and the parents or attorney can be forced to pay them under the following two conditions (20 U.S.C. § 1415(i)(3)(D)): if (a) the parents or parents' attorney files a complaint that is unreasonable and lacks a foundation or (b) the parents or parents' attorney presents a complaint for an improper purpose, such as harassing the school district or causing an unnecessary delay.

A request for hearing must address a violation or issue that has occurred within the last 2 years. In some cases, a due process hearing request can address a violation from more than 2 years ago if one of two conditions is met (20 U.S.C. §§ 1415 (f)(3)(C)–(D)): (a) the parents were prevented from requesting a due process hearing within 2 years because the school district misrepresented that it had resolved the problem or (b) the parents were prevented from requesting a due process hearing within 2 years because the school district withheld information it was required by law to share.

Another reason why it is so important to be represented by an attorney who specializes in education law is that the request must discuss all potential concerns that the parents have because, once received, any new claims can be changed only if the school district agrees in writing or if the hearing officer agrees to the amendment (20 U.S.C. § 1415(c)(2)(E)). If an amendment occurs, the timelines for the hearing are reestablished. Within 10 calendar days of receiving the request for the hearing, the school district must reply. In the reply, district officials must explain why they took the action they did, identify what other options the IEP team considered and why they were rejected, and describe the information the district officials depended on to make their decision (20 U.S.C. § 1415(c) (2)(B)).

After a due process hearing request is made, the school district must, within 15 calendar days, convene a meeting with the parents, relevant members of the IEP team, and a school district representative who has decision-making authority. (The school district cannot bring an attorney to this meeting unless the parents have an attorney as well.) This "resolution session" must take place unless both the parents and the school district waive the meeting and agree to mediation instead (20 U.S.C. § 1415(f)(B)). After receiving the complaint, the school district must try to resolve the issues through the resolution process within 30 calendar days. If the parents are unwilling to participate in the resolution process, this may delay the due process hearing, which cannot take place until the resolution session is held. Also, if the parents do not participate in the resolution session, the school district may ask a hearing officer, after the end of the 30-day period, to dismiss the parents' request for a due process hearing. If the issues are settled during the resolution deliberations, the parents and the school district must sign a legally binding agreement that is enforceable in court. Both sides then are given 3 business days to change or cancel the agreement (20 U.S.C. § 1415(f)(B)(iii)).

If the resolution process fails, the due process hearing timelines begin, and the hearing and a decision by the hearing officer are required to be completed within 45 calendar days (20 U.S.C. § 1415(f)(B)(ii)).

CHILDREN WITH DISABILITIES, AGE BIRTH TO 3 YEARS

Under federal law, services are available to a child with one or more disabilities before he or she can qualify for special education at age 3. An "infant or toddler with a disability" qualifies as deserving services if the child is less than age 3 years of age and needs early intervention because he or she is experiencing developmental delays, as measured by appropriate diagnostic instruments and procedures in at least one of the following areas (20 U.S.C. § 1432(5))—cognitive development, physical development, communication development, social or emotional development, and/or adaptive development—or has a diagnosed physical or mental condition that has a high probability of resulting in a developmental delay.

Every child has a right to obtain screening for early intervention services. An evaluation assesses the child's progress in the five areas of development listed in the preceding paragraph, assesses his or her unique strengths and needs, and identifies the services necessary to meet those needs (20 U.S.C. § 1436(a)(1)). Input from the family must be considered, including the identification of the supports and services necessary to enhance their capacity to meet the child's developmental needs (20 U.S.C. § 1436(a)(2)).

Within a reasonable time period after the evaluation is completed, an individualized family service plan (IFSP) is developed by a multidisciplinary team that includes the parents (20 U.S.C. § 1436(a)(3)). The written IFSP must contain the following details:

- a statement of the child's present levels of physical, cognitive, communication, social or emotional, and adaptive development, based on objective criteria;
- a statement of the family's resources, priorities, and concerns relating to enhancing the development of the family's child with a disability;
- a statement of the measurable results or outcomes expected to be achieved, including preliteracy and language skills, as developmentally

appropriate for the child, and the criteria, procedures, and timelines used to determine the degree to which progress toward achieving the results or outcomes is being made and whether the results or outcomes or services need to be modified or revised;

- a statement of specific early intervention services based on peer-reviewed research, to the extent practicable, necessary to meet the unique needs of the infant or toddler and the family, including the frequency, intensity, and method of delivering services;
- a statement of the natural environments in which early intervention services will appropriately be provided, including a justification of the extent, if any, to which the services will not be provided in a natural environment;
- the projected dates for initiation of services and their anticipated duration and frequency;
- the identification of the service coordinator from the profession most immediately relevant to the child's needs (or who is otherwise qualified to carry out all applicable responsibilities) who will be responsible for the implementation of the plan and coordination with other agencies and persons, including transition service; and
- the steps to be taken to support the transition of the child with a disability to preschool or other appropriate services. (20 U.S.C. § 1436(d))

The contents of the IFSP must be fully explained to the parents, and informed written consent must be obtained from the parents before early intervention services can be provided. If the parents do not provide consent with respect to a particular early intervention service, then only the early intervention services for which consent has been obtained shall be provided (20 U.S.C. § 1436(e)). The IFSP must be reviewed at least every 6 months and be rewritten every year (20 U.S.C. § 1436(b)).

The IFSP could specify that the following services could be provided (20 U.S.C. § 1432(4)(E)):

- family training, counseling, and all visits;
- special instruction;
- speech language therapy;
- occupational or physical therapy;

- psychological services;
- service coordination assistance;
- medical services for diagnostic or evaluation purposes;
- early identification, screening, and assessment services;
- health services necessary to enable the child to benefit from other early intervention services;
- social work services;
- vision services;
- assistive technology devices and services; and/or
- transportation needed for family and child to receive early intervention services.

Coordination with agencies and individuals to ensure that services are provided is the job of the *family service coordinator* (20 U.S.C. § 1436(d) (7)). Disagreements about early intervention services are resolved in one of two ways: As discussed earlier, parents can engage in either mediation (20 U.S.C. § 1439(a)(8)) or pursue the administrative hearing process (20 U.S.C. § 1439(a)(1)).

SECTION 504 OF THE REHABILITATION ACT

All programs that receive federal funding, including schools, must not discriminate against people on the basis of disability. Congress intended that the Rehabilitation Act of 1973 would remove barriers so that people with disabilities could fully participate in activities such as school (Definitions, 34 C.F.R. § 104.3(k)(2) (2010)). Section 504 of this law defines a *disability* as an impairment that substantially limits a major life activity (Definitions, 34 C.F.R. § 104.3(j)(1)(i) (2010)). As we have noted, Section 504 establishes a broader definition of disability than does IDEIA, and thus many more children qualify for services under the former legislation than the latter. School districts are financially more at risk for not complying with Section 504 than with IDEIA:

> When civil rights violations of students with disabilities is demonstrated, any federal funds can be pulled, whereas under IDEIA, only those specific IDEIA funds will be revoked for violations . . .

a [lawsuit] from a civil rights violation could potentially affect a
school district at a much broader level, including within general
education itself. (Schraven & Jolly, 2010, p. 429)

Under Section 504, school districts are required to identify students
who may have disabilities and evaluate the extra support those students
might need in order to obtain an education. School districts must use
valid assessment tools that are administered by trained people and tai-
lored to test the specific questions at hand so that the results accurately
reflect the child's needs (Evaluation and Placement, 34 C.F.R. § 104.35(a)
(2010)). No specific timelines for the district to finish the evaluation are
established by law. Parents and other education advocates may initiate
the evaluation for Section 504 services. Parental consent is not required
to conduct an initial Section 504 evaluation.

Section 504 requires periodic reevaluation of the children who receive
services under that law, although reevaluation has to occur only once
every 3 years (Evaluation and Placement, 34 C.F.R. § 104.35(a) (2010)).
Section 504 also requires a reevaluation if the school district proposes
significant changes to the child's services. Unfortunately, Section 504 fails
to require that the plan be established in writing. Nor is there clarity about
the membership of the team that makes decisions regarding placement
and services, based on the evaluation data, and the resources that may be
available within the district. Parents and consulting psychologists are not
precluded from being part of the 504 team (Evaluation and Placement,
34 C.F.R. § 104.35(c)(3) (2010)). The plan may include a broad range
of services (Nonacademic Services 34 C.F.R. §§ 104.37, 104.43–104.47
(2010)). Unless an IEP or Section 504 plan requires that services be ren-
dered in another setting, the child must be educated in the school that he
or she would attend if not disabled, and he or she must be incorporated
into mainstream classroom activities (Educational Setting, 34 C.F.R.
§ 104.34(a) (2010)).

Section 504 requires that school districts develop dispute-resolution
procedures, such as notice, an opportunity for parents to examine relevant records, an impartial hearing with the opportunity for participation by parents and representation by counsel, and a review procedure

(Procedural Safeguards, 34 C.F.R. § 104.36 (2010)). As we noted earlier, each district must have a written set of its procedures and an identified Section 504 coordinator.

CONCLUSION

An understanding of the laws governing special education is necessary to ensure that an evaluation used to help determine a child's eligibility for special education services or accommodations meets the criteria set forth by federal and state statutes. These laws—Section 504 of the Rehabilitation Act of 1973 (Nondiscrimination on the Basis of Handicap, 34 C.F.R. § 104 (2010)) and IDEIA— define concepts such as disability as they pertain to educational settings and set forth the requirements to protect children from discrimination. It is important for psychologists to be familiar with not only the definitions of key concepts but also the processes used to determine eligibility and to manage disagreements between families and schools. Psychologists who are familiar with the laws that govern special education, the processes used to determine eligibility, and how to work within the school environment are in a good position to conduct useful and helpful evaluations. Such evaluations can facilitate the work of the school team and family as they collaborate in developing an environment in which the child will be successful.

3

Referral, Clinical Interview, and Psychological Assessment

As readers will see throughout our description of conducting educational evaluations, we urge that psychologists include steps within their evaluation process that will lead the child, family, and school personnel to recognize the objectivity and fairness of the process. In this and the subsequent chapters about the evaluation process, we provide a detailed outline of the progressive steps evaluators can follow. In this chapter, we describe how psychologists can prepare and conduct the interview with the family and the psychological assessment with the child. First we describe the steps for evaluations that were initiated by the family, and then we describe minor modifications to these steps that follow from a referral issued by a school district.

A referral for an evaluation to assist with educational planning generally comes in one of three ways: (a) parent initiated, (b) attorney initiated at the parent's request, and (c) school district initiated. Regardless of the source of the referral, it is paramount that the psychologist follow a standardized,

http://dx.doi.org/10.1037/14318-004
Educational Evaluations of Children With Special Needs: Clinical and Forensic Considerations, by D. Breiger, K. Bishop, and G. A. H. Benjamin

structured approach that emphasizes transparency and objectivity. Several typical scenarios, and their possible implications for the referral process, are discussed in the following sections.

Parents may request an outside evaluation for many reasons, each of which arises from a different context. The first of these can be thought of as *Seeking Help:* Parents may feel they would benefit from additional information provided by an outside expert for many reasons—for example, diagnostic questions, the perceived complexity of the child's presentation, expertise regarding the child's condition (e.g., autism, mild traumatic head injury), recommendations from a physician or health care professional for an evaluation, the child's lack of academic progress, or the child's transition to new program. With Seeking Help types of referrals, the parents usually have had a discussion with the child's teacher and perhaps others in the school, and both sides have endorsed proceeding with an outside evaluation. The Seeking Help scenario is the most straightforward of referrals psychologists receive. The school district and the family typically appear to be working together, and little, if any, conflict is apparent.

The second type of referral appears similar to Seeking Help but is different in important aspects and can be thought of as *Seeking Consultation.* In this situation, the school district and family have experienced ongoing issues regarding the child's academic program for reasons such as qualification status, rate of academic progress, details of an individualized education plan (IEP), Section 504 plan, or disagreements regarding recommendations made by professionals outside of the school. In Seeking Consultation referrals, the psychologist is asked to consult with the school and family in order to provide information that would help reconcile the differences. The school district may have suggested seeking outside consultation to avoid litigation, and/or the parents may have indicated that they may initiate redress through the processes identified in the Individuals With Disabilities Education Improvement Act of 2004 (IDEIA) or the Americans With Disabilities Act of 1990. The parents also may contact an attorney or seek another advocate if outside consultation is not undertaken. The level of animosity between the parties can vary from mild to extreme, depending on the length of time the disagreements have lasted as well as variables such as the school district's communication skills, the quality of the academic program, and interpersonal characteristics of the parents. Typically, the school district proposes possible outside evaluators, but there may be mistrust on the parents' part that psychologists recommended by the school district would be biased in favor of the school. Parents are often concerned about releasing their child's records to the consultant because they worry that the records will negatively influence the consultant against the child. Seeking Consultation referrals have considerable risk for becoming very contentious. The use of a standardized approach that emphasizes the objectivity of the psychologist, as we describe later in this chapter, will lead to the best outcomes.

The third scenario could be called *Seeking Resolution,* and it occurs when the relationship between the school and the parents has reached the point at which attorneys are involved. The parents and the school district are seeking a resolution that will lead to the implementation of a program or support the position of one of the parties. This type of case often leads to an administrative hearing in front of an administrative law judge and involves the psychologist testifying. Seeking Resolution referrals entail the highest degree of expressed animosity by the parents and involve attorneys who often attempt to influence the psychologist's evaluation and recommendations. In the Seeking Resolution scenario, the referral could come from either the parent's attorney or the school district's attorney. This type of referral can be the most stressful for the psychologist, especially if the procedures outlined in this chapter are not followed.

Across all scenarios, the parent-initiated referral comes in different forms. The parents may have engaged an attorney who is working behind the scenes and not initially revealed to the psychologist. Another possibility is that the parents contact a psychologist to complete an evaluation as a second opinion, typically following an assessment by the school district due to disagreements with the findings. In order to guard against surprises, the psychologist should always inquire as to whether the family is working with an attorney and clarify the goals of the evaluation.

The procedures followed by the psychologist are nearly identical regardless of the referral source or the apparent scenario on initial presentation (i.e., Seeking Help, Seeking Consultation, or Seeking Resolution). The modifications in the process are minor and have to do with permission to contact one party (when initiated by school) and the number of feedback sessions (which varies according to the level of rancor between parties).

In the following sections, we describe the process for responding to a family-initiated independent educational evaluation (IEE) request. This is followed by a shorter section, in which we detail the differences in procedures when the referral for an IEE is initiated by the school district.

STEPS IN THE EVALUATION PROCESS

The following 12 procedures are described in detail in this section:

1. Accept the referral.
2. Prepare for the first clinical interviews with the family and child.
3. Review and modify the structured interview.
4. Prepare the release-of-information forms.
5. Provide nonconfidentiality warnings and complete the disclosure process.
6. Describe the process of evaluation and the role of the evaluator.
7. Administer the semistructured interview.
8. Complete the release-of-information forms.
9. Administer questionnaires to the parents and psychological testing to the child.
10. Interview teachers, school personnel, and other collateral individuals.
11. Obtain records for later review.
12. Review and integrate data immediately afterward.

1. Accept the Referral

The request for an evaluation typically is made through a phone call from the family to the psychologist. During this phone call the evaluator will gather other referral information, including

- the reason for the IEE, and the child's educational history;
- the child's assessment history;
- involvement of attorneys;
- whether there are any required evaluation domains;

- the timeline for completion of evaluation; and
- the names of important contact individuals, including teachers, for subsequent interviews.

We recommend that the psychologist have already written out the concrete steps of the typical IEE evaluation (see Appendix B), charges a flat rate for the evaluation, and be able to convey to the parents those steps and the cost of the evaluation during that initial call.

School districts are mandated under IDEIA to consider IEEs provided by parents. Parents expect that the results of the IEE will provide support for qualification for special education services. Often in such cases, a history of conflict exists between the family and the school district, or concerns have arisen about the school district not providing what the child needs. This places the psychologist in a situation that can lead to conflict with the family or the school, depending on the evaluation results (Ernst, Pelletier, & Simpson, 2008).

To minimize the conflict, the psychologist, at the onset of contact with the family, should discuss with them how the role of the evaluator is to help provide information regarding the child's functioning in order to help both the parents and the school better understand the child. Ernst et al. (2008) recommended that the psychologist directly state that the purpose of the evaluation is to determine the child's strengths and to identify the particular weaknesses that affect the child's educational functioning. In addition, the psychologist should explain that the school district is obligated to consider the results of the IEE and may accept all of the findings and recommendations, a portion of the findings and recommendations, or none of the findings and recommendations. Having this discussion at the outset can minimize misunderstandings and clarify that the psychologist is not being employed as an advocate for the parent's position.

Some parents are reluctant to give the psychologist permission to obtain school records and speak with representatives of the school or, sometimes, to obtain records of previous evaluations or contact professionals who may have important information regarding the child's functioning (e.g., physical or occupational therapists, physicians). Parents may be concerned that the information obtained may bias the psychologist, so they may want to restrict information that is disclosed to the psychologist. In order to undertake a reliable and valid evaluation, however, the psychologist needs access to records that are relevant to the assessment question. This necessitates a review of previous evaluations, contact with school officials, and access to other records that reflect on the child's condition. The psychologist is guided in this by the American Psychological Association's (2002, 2010) Standard 9.01, Bases for Assessments, which maintains that psychologists' assessments, recommendations, reports, and psychological diagnostic or evaluative statements are based on information and techniques (including personal interviews of the individual when appropriate) sufficient to provide appropriate substantiation for their findings (also see Standards 2.04, Bases for Scientific and Professional Judgments, and 9.06, Interpreting Assessment Results; http://www.apa.org/ethics/code/index.aspx).

The psychologist should explain that the school is likely to use all of the data at its disposal if a conflict arises. Integration of all of the data by the IEE will likely increase the credibility of the evaluation and provide an opportunity to explain fully the nuances that emerge from a complicated set of data. Such an explanation about complete access to all of the information and how the psychologist will use the information usually reassures the family. If the family continues to refuse to grant the psychologist access to information he or she believes is necessary to complete a valid and reliable evaluation, then the psychologist should decline to conduct the evaluation. Without having accessed the needed data, the psychologist may later face an ethical complaint or a lawsuit for negligence, or both.

- At this point in the phone call, the psychologist will indicate whether he or she will be able to accept the referral.
- It is necessary to have required records to review before interviewing the family. This can be facilitated by sending completed release-of-information forms to the family with self-addressed return envelopes. The psychologist can also schedule an appointment with family to complete the forms at his or her office.
- The appointment for the interview and psychological assessment is scheduled.

After the initial phone call, it would behoove the psychologist to forward to the family details about the steps of the likely evaluation process (see Appendix C), a record of what the family has requested, and a description of the cost for those services. The psychologist also could provide a tentative appointment for a feedback session with the family to discuss the findings, but he or she should temper the commitment by suggesting that the schedule will depend on obtaining documentation from the school and compliance from the family in a timely manner.

2. Prepare for the First Clinical Interviews With the Family and Child

The evaluator should review all available records before the interview with the family. This will enable him or her to prepare so that the evaluation process is targeted and sequenced in a manner that will facilitate a valid and reliable process.

3. Review and Modify the Structured Interview

Before meeting with the family and child, the psychologist should review the child's school record, medical record, and the referral questions from the school and then map out the specific evaluation process. We recommend that the interview questions for both the parents and child be within the context of a semistructured interview so that the evaluator can record answers contemporaneously. Such an approach will increase the validity of the evaluation process by reducing clinical judgment errors due to inaccuracies resulting from (Garb, 1989, 2005) overreliance on memory, confirmatory and hindsight bias, and overreliance on unique data.

4. Prepare the Release-of-Information Forms

After reviewing the school record, the evaluator may be able to identify in advance individuals who can provide relevant information (i.e., collaterals who can be interviewed to gain additional information that will help the evaluator understand more about the child, e.g., teachers). Filling out the necessary sections of the release-of-information forms in advance can save time for the evaluator and increase the likelihood of gaining permission from the parents.

5. Provide Nonconfidentiality Warnings and Complete the Disclosure Process

Upon arrival in the clinic, the family should have already reviewed the steps of the evaluation process (see Appendix C), including the written disclosure about confidentiality and mandatory reporting duties. Fees should be paid at this time. The family and child (depending on the child's age) sign the disclosure form (see Appendix B) that establishes that the party has consented to the confidentiality waiver and agrees to proceed with the evaluation. Although the family may have already signed a consent and release-of-information form provided by the school, the evaluator must engage in this process too. This presents another opportunity to discuss the implications of disclosure and release of information as well as additional information, such as limits of confidentiality with the family and, when appropriate, the child.

The disclosure form must include an explanation of the purpose of the evaluation and inform the family and child that they have the right to decline to respond to any questions. The family also should be informed that information gathered from all sources through the evaluation may be presented in verbal or written form to the school district. This warning is given before information is collected from the parties, their children, and individuals who serve as collateral sources.

The following is an example of what the evaluator might say at the beginning of the meeting:

> I am a psychologist, and I am conducting an independent educational evaluation. My understanding is that you and the school district have agreed to this evaluation. Is that your understanding? [Wait for the party's response.] I want to tell you about some details that you have read in the disclosure statement and the steps of the evaluation process. Perhaps your lawyer also may have gone over

some of the details. In all of the interviews we have together, you do not have to answer any questions I will ask you. You do not have to answer questions on the forms I give you. If you do answer, what you say will *not* be kept confidential or private between you and me. I may use what you tell me in the evaluation report. In addition, the school district will read the evaluation report. Do you understand all that I have said? [Wait for the party's response.] Can you tell me in your own words what I just said? [Wait for the party's response; restate if the party's response does not reflect understanding about nonconfidentiality and freedom to decline answers.] Finally, we can stop this interview at any time if you need a break or want to end. Any questions? [Wait for the party's response.]

In the report, the evaluator should insert a statement reflecting that the warning of nonconfidentiality was provided, such as the following:

All parties to this evaluation were informed at the onset of all interviews that the data collected from clinical interviews, records, and collateral contacts would be used for this report to the court, or verbal testimony, or both. The parties indicated that they understood that no information would be kept confidential. The parties were aware that it was within their right to refuse to answer a question or line of questions. All parties acknowledged that they understood this information.

In some instances, a party may refuse to sign the consent agreement because of an objection to one or more of the terms of the agreement. If the party seeks advice from the evaluator about signing the disclosure form or asks for an interpretation of its legal significance, the evaluator should refer the party back to his or her school district and the party's lawyer. If the evaluator cannot obtain informed consent, the remainder of the appointment may need to be rescheduled. The evaluator should point out that the agreement is nonnegotiable. If the party contends that she or he will sign the informed consent agreement only under protest, the evaluator should terminate the appointment. At this point, the evaluator should inform the party that a letter will be sent to the school district and any attorneys involved who will request guidance. This statement should be delivered matter-of-factly, and the evaluator should explain to the party that no deviations from the standardized evaluation process are possible.

Throughout the disclosure process, regardless of the provocation, the evaluator must remain poised and courteous and speak matter-of-factly to the party. The initial interactions with a party will set the tone and tenor of the subsequent assessment proceedings. A measured stance remains critical at the onset of the evaluation and, once established, will be easier to maintain throughout the evaluation. The evaluator should maintain firm and reasonable boundaries, in particular with a suspicious, difficult individual; otherwise, the evaluator will collude with the high-conflict tactics of a party and limit the efficacy of the process.

On occasion, the parties may agree through their attorneys to changes in the disclosure agreement without consulting with the evaluator first, or a judge may order changes in the disclosure agreement. If the changes will result in exposing the evaluator to violating practices (described below) that are intended to deter ethical complaints (e.g., a lawyer alters the disclosure agreement so that psychological testing and collateral interviews are precluded), the evaluator should decline to conduct the evaluation.

6. Describe the Process of Evaluation and the Role of the Evaluator

Next, the evaluator should discuss the purpose and goals of the evaluation with the family and address any concerns they raise. In addition, he or she should discuss the elements of the evaluation process in person and hand out a written set of steps so the family can review them later.

At this juncture, the psychologist should explain the role of the evaluator in the IEE process. He or she should emphasize that evaluators are not agents of the school district or advocates for the family and explain that, instead, any findings regarding the child result from multiple-measure corroboration of the evidence that emerges during the evaluation process. The description of convergent validity and how the psychologist will use the concept throughout the process will help define the role of the evaluator as someone focused on providing objective information regarding the child that will be used by the IEP team to create an appropriate educational plan.

The feedback session will also be scheduled during the initial interview. The evaluator should discuss with the family and school officials whether the feedback session will be conducted with all parties together or with the family first and then with the school district representatives. If the latter approach is to be used, the psychologist should stress that the information presented during the feedback sessions will be the same at each session. We routinely recommend the latter approach so that family members have a chance to be better prepared for the IEP team meeting. Often, the family has an easier time accepting the findings of the evaluation if the evidence that emerged from the evaluation is heard and discussed twice.

As part of the discussion about how the findings of the evaluation will be shared, the evaluator also should explain that all information or recommendations shared with the family will also be shared with the school but that any information not relevant to the child's educational planning will not be shared with the school. Examples of such information could include recommendations for individual therapy or family therapy.

The evaluation report may include diagnostic information, intervention recommendations, and treatment recommendations. IDEIA and state special education laws prohibit evaluators from independently determining eligibility, interventions, or classroom placement. The evaluator should discuss with the family the possibility of him or her participating in future meetings (e.g., IEP meetings). The financial charges for participating in meetings and the availability of the evaluator should be discussed with both the school personnel and family at the outset.

7. Administer the Semistructured Interview

The assessment takes the form of a structured or semistructured interview. We have found semistructured interviews to be very effective. Such an interview contains sections that allow for collection of a comprehensive history, including medical history, developmental history, academic history, social history, behavioral history, and family history.

The evaluation is intended to obtain information about the child that is reliable, valid, and relevant to the academic setting. The academic relevance of recommendations, especially when informed by the collaboration from the school's personnel, can increase the credibility of the evaluation, in particular if the evaluator works outside the educational community (Kanne, Randolph, & Farmer, 2008).

A child's initial evaluation must include a variety of assessment tools to gather relevant information regarding health, developmental, functional, behavioral, and academic information. The evaluation includes information that not only is necessary for determining eligibility for services but also helps determine the child's educational needs.

The clinical interview begins with a review of identifying demographic information, including, name, date of birth, and child's grade in school. The interview then transitions to a review of why the child was referred for evaluation. This is intended as a brief review of the referral information; detailed information regarding the concerns will be collected later in the interview. Next, the concerns of the parent/informant are discussed. The evaluator can help with this discussion by suggesting that the concerns be current ones and not a repetition of previous problems with the school district. If the parent/informant begins to provide considerable historical information, they should be informed that it is easier if the examiner follows a specific interview structure that will inquire about historical information later in the interview.

The interview then transitions to a discussion of developmental factors. To decrease the informant's anxiety regarding remembering exact dates, the interviewer can say something such as the following:

> I am trying to understand your child's development and would like
> to start at the beginning. I know that it is often difficult to remember
> dates and details from many years ago, but I would like to get a general sense of your child's history. Don't worry if you can't remember
> every detail.

It is our view that the way parents/informants relay the child's history is more informative than the dates developmental milestones were met. The interviewer should be listening for themes and developing hypotheses regarding behavior that can be tested later in the interview.

We have found it helpful to preface each interview section with a brief overview of the domain being explored. For developmental factors, the following sections are covered:

- prenatal history;
- mother's health during pregnancy; age at time of pregnancy; and use of medications, prescription drugs, illicit drugs, alcohol, and tobacco;
- mother's health during delivery and immediate postnatal period;
- health and temperament of the child during the postnatal period;
- developmental history (e.g., milestones, including motor, language, and bowel and bladder control);
- medical history, including hospitalizations, and basic health issues, such as hearing, vision, coordination, and chronic illnesses;
- trauma, abuse/neglect, and drug or alcohol abuse history;
- treatment history, focusing on both medical treatment, including prescription medication history, as well as psychological treatment; and
- academic history, beginning with the first structured learning setting (e.g., preschool, day care) and proceeding through a year-by-year review, including when concerns arose; how those concerns were addressed; grades; performance on district, state, and nationally normed measures; special education evaluations, and the current academic plan.

The end of the academic history section includes a detailed discussion of current academic concerns and information regarding any ongoing disagreements with the school district.

The final section of the interview should focus on social, emotional, and behavioral functioning. This part of the semistructured interview consists of domains commonly discussed in the initial parental interview process (Sattler & Hoge, 2006). This is an opportunity for the evaluator to gather information regarding the child's behavior at home and in the community as well as the interaction between the child and his or her parents. The evaluator and parents/informants also should discuss, in detail, any other information that is necessary to help the evaluator understand behavior patterns and intervention strategies that have worked and those that have been tried in the past. This is an excellent point in the interview to ask the parents to describe a typical school day and typical weekend day beginning with when the child wakes and finishing with when the child goes to bed.

By this time in the interview, the evaluator should have covered many of the areas that relate to psychiatric diagnosis. The last section covers the diagnostic criteria for childhood onset disorders. Evaluators may want to approach this section of the interview by asking about core symptoms of a particular disorder and, if the parents deny observing the symptoms, moving on to the next disorder. Parents should also complete broadband behavior checklists (e.g., the Child Behavior Checklist [Achenbach & Rescorla, 2001], Behavior Assessment System for Children, Second Edition [BASC 2; Reynolds & Kamphaus, 2004]), which will allow for further detection of both internalizing and externalizing disorders. The evaluator also can administer additional questionnaires to evaluate potential narrow-band disorders (e.g., Children's Depression Inventory [Kovacs, 2011], Barkley Deficits in Executive Functioning Scale—Children and Adolescents [Barkley, 2012], and the Behavior Rating Inventory of Executive Function [Gioia, Isquith, Guy, & Kenworthy, 2003]). In addition, comparable questionnaires can be sent to teachers who are familiar with the student. Finally, family history is obtained for all first-degree relatives.

At the conclusion of the interview, which can take between 60 and 120 minutes, the psychologist should ask the parents whether there is anything else they would like to discuss.

8. Complete the Release-of-Information Forms

Before ending the session, the evaluator should present release-of-information forms for individuals other than the school district. These releases allow the evaluator to access records and speak to third party individuals who may be able to provide information regarding the child's functioning. Researchers have shown support for the use of multiple informants in the assessment of problem behaviors and have noted that a lack of multiple informants may lead to the type of bias issues mentioned earlier in this chapter (Kerr, Lunkenheimer, & Olson, 2007).

The evaluator should explain that she or he will contact only collaterals who can provide firsthand information about the child's functioning. Potentially informative records may include mental health records, medical records, psychological and educational testing reports, and social services agency records.

Even though some jurisdictions may not require formal releases of information, evaluators use them so that each party understands who will be contacted during the course of the evaluation. This practice supports the impression of evaluator fairness and objectivity in the minds of the parties, deters party dissembling, and saves evaluator time.

9. Administer Questionnaires to the Parents and Psychological Testing to the Child

Parent Questionnaires

The interview ends with the parents completing standardized questionnaires such as the BASC 2. This particular assessment provides both clinical and adaptive scales that provide the evaluator insight into problem behaviors and areas of clinical concern (Frick, Barry, & Kamphaus, 2010). The evaluator should explain how to complete the questionnaires, referring to the instructions in the manual, and answer any questions the parent raises. If both parents are present at the interview, they should be asked if they would prefer to complete the questionnaires together or separately. If one parent is present, the evaluator should ask whether he or she would like to take home a set of questionnaires to the spouse or other caretaker.

Psychological Testing With the Child

The evaluator should orient the child to the testing session by explaining what will happen during the session. This should be done using developmentally appropriate terms. Any use of the term *games* to describe the testing should be avoided because this can set up the child to expect that activities will be fun and that effort is not necessary. Instead, the evaluator should tell the child, in age-appropriate terms, that he or she will be asked to complete a number of activities that will help the evaluator understand what the child's strengths are and to understand whether the child has any weaknesses. We have found that telling children we will look at their language skills, memory, attention, problem solving, visual skills, motor speed, drawing, and schoolwork helps set the stage for the evaluation. Evaluators should explain that their role is to try their best to administer the tasks correctly and answer any questions the child has and that the child's job is to try his or her best on the activities.

We routinely use a symptom validity measure during the initial stage of the assessment. Symptom validity measures are used much less frequently with children than they are with adults. However, such measures are useful in identifying children who appear to have reduced motivation. The importance of identifying noncredible effort cannot be overstated. The basis for interpretation of psychological assessment data rests on the assumption the examinee responded with adequate effort and in an unbiased manner (Kirkwood, 2012). If the examinee has responded with noncredible effort, and/or attempts to exaggerate or feign symptoms, the results of the evaluation will not be a reliable or valid reflection of his or her abilities. In this case, significant problems can arise, including errors in interpretation, inaccurate diagnoses, inappropriate treatment recommendations, and inappropriate academic placement decisions. It also can cause psychological harm to examinees and their families. We have used the Test of Memory Malingering (Tombaugh, 1996) for several years and found it to be a helpful tool. The Test of Memory Malingering has been one of the best-studied symptom validity tests and has a number of strengths, including its easy use with children as young as 6, ease of administration, and empirical support. An in-depth discussion of symptom validity tests is beyond the scope of this book; interested readers can find more information in Kirkwood (2012) and Kirkwood, Yeates, Randolph, and Kirk (2012).

The choice of assessment instruments used in the evaluation is determined in part by the domains of assessment required by IDEIA, the instruments approved by the individual state's department of education, and the evaluator's clinical judgment. The information gathered during the review of records, interviews with parents, and interviews with school personnel is used to determine the domains evaluated and measures chosen.

The psychologist will not be making the diagnoses in IDEIA categories that require a medical professional for diagnoses (e.g., deafness,

deafness–blindness, hearing impairment; see Chapter 1, this volume); however, the adverse educational impact of these diagnoses is an important aspect of the assessment. Psychologists should evaluate and diagnose the other conditions that are in categories of eligibility. Many psychologists, especially those with neuropsychological training, evaluate children with medical disorders that frequently influence academic achievement (e.g., brain tumors, cancer, seizure disorders). The IDEIA definition of each area of disability is available in a variety of publications as well as online (see, e.g., http://idea.ed.gov/).

IDEIA requires that a child be evaluated in all areas of suspected disability and that the assessment tools provide relevant information that directly helps people determine the educational needs of the child. Psychologists need to be familiar with the instruments that the state education department has indicated are approved for use in special education evaluations. In addition, it is important for psychologists to be familiar with the data regarding the reliability, validity, and relation to areas of suspected disability. They should strive, however, to not overevaluate a child but instead to carefully consider how the information from each measure will help in determining the child's educational needs. This will help ensure that instruments that do not provide useful information are not used.

Areas assessed include the following:

- intelligence (cognitive abilities),
- learning and memory,
- academic achievement,
- language (expressive language, receptive language, fluency),
- visual perceptual skills,
- auditory perceptual skills,
- motor skills (gross and fine motor),
- social and emotional behavior/personality, and
- adaptive behavior.

A number of excellent references provide reviews of frequently used assessment tools, including important information regarding reliability and validity of the instruments (e.g., Baron, 2004; Sattler, 2008).

Examiners will need to be familiar with the criteria used by their state for determination of eligibility for special education. This is particularly important, for example, when a school district uses the discrepancy model for determining whether a learning disability is present. There is a significant lag between research findings published regarding definitions of terms such as *learning disabilities* and changes in state law regarding definitions. Evaluators should be aware of these differences and may need to explain the differences to both families and school personnel. The changes introduced in IDEIA in 2004 indicate that states must permit the use of a process based on the child's response to scientific, research-based intervention and may permit the use of other alternative research-based procedures for determining whether a child has a specific learning disability (20 U.S.C. § 1414 (b)(6)(B)). The evaluator will need to be familiar with how these changes may apply in the case they are assessing.

10. Interview Teachers, School Personnel, and Other Collateral Individuals

After the initial interview with the parents and child, the evaluator should review all available records before the interview with representatives from the school district. Often, multiple individuals from the school district—for example, teachers, psychologists, principals, and special education administrators—will be interviewed. The interviews are semistructured and vary depending on the individual's experience with the child.

The interview of teachers begins with the evaluator introducing him- or herself and explaining the purpose of the interview and how the information shared will be used. We find it helpful to begin the interview by asking how long the teacher has known the child, how much time he or she spends with the child, and the context of their contact. Next, the teacher is asked to describe in general how the child is doing and any concerns the teacher has regarding academic performance or behavior in the classroom. Detail about attendance, stamina, attention, activity level, perceived motivation, homework completion, and social functioning should be sought. Depending on the subject taught by the teacher, specific questions regarding reading, arithmetic, spelling, writing, language, learning/ memory, perceptual skills, and motor skills should be asked. In addition, behavior difficulties and relationships with peers and adults should be addressed. We recommend that as the interview unfolds, clarifying responses by asking for concrete descriptions of behavior that are observable and unambiguous. Other examples of the teacher's responses to the child's behavior, including any interventions, both successful and unsuccessful, also should be sought. In addition, the teacher may provide suggestions for helping the child, and a description of the child's strengths. Finally, the extent of contact the teacher has had with the child's family should be established, and suggestions about working with the family clarified. In concluding the interview, the evaluator should ask the teacher if he or she has any questions or would like to add other facts at the time. The evaluator should end the interview by letting the teacher know he or she will be sent one or more standardized questionnaires (e.g., BASC 2, Behavior Rating Inventory of Executive Function) and are given instructions about where to return them.

11. Obtain Records for Later Review

The evaluator must submit the request for records to the different collaterals. If the records are not received in approximately two weeks, the evaluator should contact the parents and instruct them to ask the agency or individual to send the requested records.

12. Review and Integrate Data Immediately Afterward

The standardized collection of data can be further strengthened by drafting the preliminary report on the same day that the evaluator meets with the family and child for the subsequent feedback interview (see Chapter 4). This practice reduces errors in clinical judgment.

At the feedback interview, give the family the opportunity to clarify the drafted version of the clinical interview, including the direct statements of the parents that were used to create an ideographic narrative that represents the characteristics of how the child operates. Parents are more likely to feel heard if their voices are quoted accurately and can see that the evaluator has accurately described what they have reported. The evaluator should ask the parents to return the additions to the drafted version of the clinical interview within 1 week, and the evaluator should incorporate those additions into the next draft of the report.

Data from the interviews and testing will help ascertain contributing factors associated with functional aspects of the child's behaviors and the developmental and educational needs of the child. After collecting and scoring of all the data, the psychologist should identify areas that need clarity, for example, achievement measures, missing data, inconsistent data from direct assessments with previous assessments, and patterns suggesting poor effort/motivation. Whenever inconsistent data are obtained, the psychologist should recheck the scoring of the instruments. Scoring errors are common and can occur with both hand-scored instruments and computerized scoring programs. When significant discrepancies occur among the data collected by the psychologist and other evaluators, it is best to obtain the raw scores from the other evaluations. One possible explanation is that the statistical relationships between measures used may be different from the data obtained from the measures used in other evaluations. For example, such an issue has emerged when a measure has been restandardized (e.g., the Wechsler Intelligence Scale for Children— Third Edition [Wechsler, 1991] and the Wechsler Intelligence Scale for Children—Fourth Edition [Wechsler, 2004]).

After reviewing the data, the psychologist may decide to schedule additional testing, administer additional measures to be completed by informants, and/or schedule and complete follow-up interviews. Emerging hypotheses about the findings that would result from the evidence can further be explored by interviews with significant collateral reporters, such as earlier evaluators, teachers, interventionists, and health care professionals. Each collateral contact should be followed up with a written summary on the day of the interview so that the details and nuances of what the collateral observed or reported about the child can be accurately recorded in the evaluation report. This process also will minimize clinical judgment errors.

We have found, in custody evaluations, that to further increase the reliability of the evidence a narrative summary of collateral interviews should be forwarded to the collateral before the day of the interview to make additions and provide a further check for accuracy of the interview data. This part of the process increases transparency and models team respect. As soon as each collateral interview is completed, the evaluator should inform the collateral reporter that, later in the day, a written summary of the interview will be faxed or electronically mailed for review. Such a review also deters a collateral from complaining later that the evaluator misrepresented or failed to insert details that might affect the outcome of the evaluation. The approach also ensures that collaterals believe they were fairly and thoroughly understood and produces a contemporaneous record of collateral's satisfaction with the results of the interview. The final report incorporates any additions the collaterals have made. This approach, although not commonly used in evaluations other than custody evaluations, is occasionally useful to consider in IEEs as well.

INDEPENDENT EDUCATIONAL EVALUATION REQUESTED BY THE SCHOOL DISTRICT

The process for school district–initiated evaluations is the same as outlined above for parent-initiated IEEs, with some minor differences, which we highlight below.

The evaluator is contacted by the school to determine whether an assessment is possible and to discuss the terms of the contractual arrangement. During the call, the psychologist should make note of what the school representative has requested and afterward forward the steps of the likely evaluation process to the school (see Appendix C) as well as clarify the cost for those services.

During the initial meeting with school officials, the evaluator should gather other referral information, including

- the reason for the IEE, and the child's educational history;
- assessment history;

- involvement of attorneys;
- whether there are any required evaluation domains;
- the timeline for completion of evaluation; and
- the names of important contact individuals, including teachers, for subsequent interviews.

The evaluator could also provide a tentative date for a feedback session with school personnel and the family to discuss findings but should temper the commitment by suggesting that the schedules depend on obtaining documentation from the school and compliance from the family in a timely manner.

The evaluator should ask school officials to provide the family's contact information and the date by which the child's educational file will be sent. Such a commitment provides a written record from the school that can be depended on so that the family involved will not be frustrated by having to reschedule the initial meeting because their child's record did not arrive in a timely manner. The communication also demonstrates that the psychologist reasonably relied on the school's engagement with the family and on the school obtaining a release from the family to go forward with the evaluation.

Once the school district has obtained consent from the family to release their personal information and has passed this along to the evaluator, the evaluator should contact the family to schedule the first meeting with them. The details from this point forward are the same as described earlier in this chapter.

CASE EXAMPLE

SW[1] is a 10-year-old boy who was referred by his school district for an IEE. He is having significant difficulty in school due to internalizing behaviors, externalizing behaviors, and poor academic performance. The school district had recommended an IEE because they were concerned that SW's behavior was deteriorating and he did not seem to be responding to

[1]Here and elsewhere, case examples have been disguised to protect client confidentiality.

interventions they had implemented. The school district was concerned that there were factors outside of school that were contributing to his difficulties. The representative of the school district indicated that SW's mother was comfortable with the evaluation and had given permission for the psychologist to contact her and that she had signed a release form allowing the school to send her son's school records to the psychologist. The school was requesting a comprehensive evaluation to include assessment of the following areas: cognitive, academic, neuropsychological, and social/emotional functioning.

SW's mother initially was reluctant to authorize consent to release records from her son's pediatrician, who had carried out several medication trials. Ms. W was divorced, and she reported that SW's father did not feel anything was wrong with SW and was not supportive of the evaluation. She indicated that she was concerned with her child being labeled and expressed concern that because the school district was paying for the evaluation the psychologist would, in essence, be working for the school district. The psychologist reviewed with Ms. W the importance of obtaining information necessary to complete a thorough evaluation and emphasized that information would be obtained from the pediatrician, not given to the pediatrician, and that no information would be released to the physician without her consent. When discussing Ms. W's concern regarding bias, the psychologist indicated that the district was paying for an evaluation, not an opinion. The issue of concern regarding labeling frequently comes up, and there is no simple way to respond. In this case, the psychologist discussed with Ms. W the importance of understanding her son in order to make the best recommendations possible. In addition, the psychologist observed that the teachers and other children were aware that SW was having problems and that a "label" would not change that but could help the teacher and school staff better understand her son. After this discussion, Ms. W agreed to proceed with the evaluation and willingly signed the forms giving the psychologist permission to contact her son's pediatrician.

A phone call to the pediatrician revealed a narrative different from the one Ms. W had presented. The pediatrician reported that the medication trials had all been stopped due to Ms. W's anxiety regarding her child's taking medicine. Ms. W had indicated that the trials were stopped because SW either did not benefit from the medicine or experienced significant side effects. The information provided by the pediatrician indicated that SW had not actually had an adequate treatment trial. The pediatrician indicated a willingness to work with Ms. W as well as cooperate with other professionals involved in SW's care.

When psychologists are comfortable that sufficient data have been collected to answer the referral questions, preparation for feedback begins. This is the topic of the next chapter.

Concluding Evaluation and Feedback

All aspects of the evaluation are necessary, but the feedback session at the conclusion of the evaluation is particularly important. Despite the importance of providing feedback, surprisingly little has been written in the psychology literature about it. *Feedback* has been described as a "dynamic, interactive process" (Pope, 1992, p. 268). The American Psychological Association's (2002, 2010) "Ethical Principles of Psychologists and Code of Conduct" indicates that the psychologist must take reasonable steps to provide feedback unless the nature of the relationship precludes providing feedback (Standard 9.10, Explaining Assessment Results; http://www.apa.org/ethics/code/index.aspx?item=12). The degree to which aspects of feedback are addressed varies by state as well as by professional

http://dx.doi.org/10.1037/14318-005
Educational Evaluations of Children With Special Needs: Clinical and Forensic Considerations, by D. Breiger, K. Bishop, and G. A. H. Benjamin

organization. For example, the American Academy of Clinical Neuro-psychology (2007) practice guidelines state:

> Feedback regarding the evaluation findings and recommendations [is] provided in a manner that is comprehensible to intended recipients and which respects the well-being, dignity, and rights of the individual examinee. Ethical and legal guidelines pertaining to the provision of feedback should be identified and followed. (p. 226)

Two options exist for providing feedback to parents and school officials. One option is for the psychologist to be involved in two separate feedback sessions, one with the parents and one with the school district; the second option is for the psychologist to conduct one single session with the family and representatives from the school district. We recommend talking about these options with parents and considering their preference. Before scheduling the feedback session, the psychologist should discuss the different aspects of the session with the parents, including who will attend, the length of the meeting, what will happen during the meeting, what material will be discussed, and the school district's level of involvement.

Both options have advantages and disadvantages. Meeting with the family first provides the following six benefits: (a) an opportunity to discuss sensitive issues that may not be germane to the goals of the evaluation (e.g., recommendations for parent training); (b) a more leisurely meeting so that the family has time to ask questions in a private setting and not feel rushed into making decisions; (c) time to process with the family the recommendations that will be made to the school and how they might affect the child; (d) involvement of the child, or a discussion of how to convey the information to the child; (e) a lower level of stress than a large group meeting would entail and an increased chance that the parents will understand the assessment results and recommendations; and (f) the opportunity to prepare the parents better for the larger feedback session and thereby facilitate their participation in the larger team meetings.

Meeting with school officials after meeting with the family also has advantages. The psychologist can inquire about issues raised during the meeting with the family without concern for the sensitivity of the family members, and school officials can ask the psychologist questions in a more private setting and digest information during a professional meeting that may involve less posturing about the school's legal position.

On the other hand, meeting with the family first does have disadvantages, such as the following two: (a) the family may not think to raise issues that will become apparent when meeting subsequently with school officials, and (b) families and school officials may report different perceptions of the feedback. Similarly, meeting with school officials after first meeting with the family can include the following two disadvantages: (a) school officials may report a different perception of the feedback to the family than was the psychologist's intention; and (b) school officials may begin to formulate interventions for the student without receiving adequate input from the family and student, which likely will lead to the family feeling betrayed or disrespected.

Regarding the second option, meeting with family and school officials together, advantages include the facts that everyone hears the information at same time, everyone has an opportunity to hear all questions and answers, and misunderstandings can be reduced if information is summarized at the end of the meeting. There are disadvantages too. The family may feel embarrassed, blamed, or betrayed when sensitive information regarding the family and/or student in the evaluation report is discussed in front of the group; individuals may feel uncomfortable disclosing information in front of each other; and previous conflict between family and school personnel may interfere with the presentation of material.

We have found that conducting the feedback session with parents prior to providing feedback to the school is preferred by most parents. It allows for sensitive or private material to be discussed in a safe environment and for the psychologist to make recommendations that may not be part of the educational evaluation. For example, information may have been obtained during the evaluation that leads the psychologist to suggest that the family consider treatment with a psychologist. This may be valuable to the parents, but it is not something that is germane to the goals of the educational evaluation.

THE PROCESS OF PROVIDING FEEDBACK

Psychologists who evaluate children for special education services or accommodations need a variety of skills and prerequisite knowledge. They may be approached by parents who are seeking help in understanding their child and who are not seeking services from the public school or are not aware of what services may be available. Alternatively, a psychologist might be contacted by an attorney representing a family that is in conflict with a school district and may have asked for an independent educational evaluation (IEE) at public expense or as part of a due process hearing. Those are the extremes; most situations lie between them. Some of the prerequisites for successful work in this area are knowledge of laws that govern special education and Section 504 accommodations, familiarity with the rules under which school districts operate, familiarity with school environments, well-developed evaluation skills, and thoughtfully used clinical skills.

The feedback sessions provide an opportunity for psychologists to present their findings and recommendations as well as to elicit comments from the family and school district representatives. A successful session is one in which all parties understand the findings and have an opportunity for their questions to be answered and to discuss an outline for the child's future academic plan.

It is not uncommon that individuals participate in the feedback session who were not present during the initial or subsequent interviews (e.g., parent, relative, friend, advocate). We believe that the outline provided below will be sufficiently informative for new members who come to the meeting. We know of no specific guidelines regarding the participation of the child in the feedback session. It has been our experience that children under age 13 do not participate in the session because, quite typically, they are not developmentally equipped to process the data. However, this issue should be discussed with the parents at the time the feedback session is scheduled.

We have provided feedback to younger children in several ways, including inviting them into the parent session after the session has been completed, or scheduling a separate session for the child and the parents at a different time. We urge that psychologists speak with the parents about how they will discuss the results and recommendations with the child in an age- and developmentally appropriate manner. We do encourage adolescents to participate in the feedback session. There are special considerations when the child or adolescent is participating in the meeting (American Academy of Clinical Neuropsychology, 2007; Pope, 1992). Be sure to consider the possible negative or detrimental impact of feedback on individuals who are not developmentally or cognitively able to understand the information and may misconstrue it. We have found that the following eight steps work well:

1. Indicate that the session is a working meeting and that a rigid script will not be followed.
2. Encourage the participants to make comments, ask questions, and if they disagree with what they hear, to express this disagreement.
3. Introduce the general framework for the session.
4. Provide an opportunity to learn about anything new that has arisen since the last contact with the psychologist (e.g., changes in medical status, educational status, emotional status, new results from other examinations).
5. Review the purpose of the evaluation as well as the issues of disclosure and confidentiality.
6. Describe the methodology of the evaluation and areas of assessment so that individuals present who did not participate in the initial interviews can understand the foundation on which the findings rest.
7. Discuss the results of the evaluation and the evidence that supports each finding.
8. Discuss recommendations and next steps.

Feedback is a process, not simply a dry exercise in presenting data. We often let participants know that the feedback session is not a lecture and that we have not prepared a PowerPoint presentation for them to suffer through.

It is helpful to ask parents what questions they would like addressed. This helps the psychologist organize the feedback session and reduces the likelihood that the family's questions will not be addressed. It also alerts the psychologist to issues that may not have been the focus of his or her preparations for the feedback session and that may have arisen since the earlier meeting.

Before discussing the results, we recommend providing a description of the child's behavior during the testing session. This is a summary of the information that is included in the "Behavior Observations" section of the report. The description should include the child's observed mood, level of cooperation, perceived level of motivation, and concrete examples of aspects of attention. Any unusual or atypical behaviors should also be reviewed. If the child is participating in the feedback session, we use developmentally appropriate terms and inquire as to whether the child has any questions regarding any of the activities he or she completed and whether he or she agrees with our description of the behaviors during the testing session. We find it helpful to then ask the parents whether the description of their child's behavior is consistent with their experience. This discussion establishes a foundation for introducing the concepts of reliability and validity of the data. We then recommend that a summary statement be made at that time about the psychologist's confidence in the reliability and validity of the findings.

We begin the discussion of the results (Step 7) with what we call the "big picture," that is, general impressions and findings. We indicate that the reason we start with the big picture is so "that way, you won't be sitting on the edge of your seat" or "You won't be waiting for the other shoe to drop." For example, statements such as "Consistent with what you already know, your child has difficulty reading, and our results indicate that she has a reading disability or, as it is often called, 'dyslexia'" can begin this portion of the feedback session. After the major findings and themes have been introduced, the psychologist should discuss the findings in more detail, using handouts or other materials he or she finds helpful.

Next, the child's scores from the test measures and descriptions of levels of performance are discussed (also Step 7). There is considerable evidence from psychology research that the language used to convey information and the way the information is introduced can have a significant influence on the understanding of the information (Kahneman,

2011; Pope, 1992). In addition, researchers have noted that the complexity of language used in psychological reports leads to a lack of readability for clients and may decrease the utility of the reports (Brenner, 2003; Harvey, 2006; Mastoras, Climie, McCrimmon, & Schwean, 2011). This is not surprising given that psychological tests use a variety of terms to describe a child's performance, for example, *standard scores, percentiles,* and *grade and age equivalents,* in addition to terms such as *average, below average,* and so on. Frequently, different measures will use different cutoff scores for the same descriptor. We urge that psychologists discuss the scores in a way that will help the participants understand the child's performance. One way to do this is to use examples such as, "Your child performed in the average range, or around the 50th percentile. That means that she did as well as 50 out of 100 children the same age (in the same grade)." Use caution when discussing age or grade equivalents. Sattler (2008) provided a detailed explanation of the limitations of grade and age equivalents. He pointed out that age and grade equivalents should be interpreted carefully because they can be easily misinterpreted, for a number of reasons. For example, they encourage comparisons between inappropriate groups (Sattler, 2008); for example, if a child in third grade has a grade equivalent in math of 5.2, it means that the third-grader obtained the same number correct as an average fifth-grader on the test; it does not mean that both children possess the same overall mathematical skills. Grade and age equivalents suggest that growth is a constant throughout the year, which is not the case.

If the psychologist has reviewed the results of other assessments (e.g., evaluations by school district officials and/or other experts), Step 7 will also contain a review of the results and how the current results compare with previous evaluations. Concluding this section is a review of the major findings as well as a presentation of diagnostic impressions and a discussion of what, if any, conditions appear to be met for qualification for specially designed instruction (special education services) and/or accommodations (i.e., Section 504). The evaluator should ask participants if they have questions or would like clarification of any of the details before moving to a discussion of the recommendations.

Before discussing the recommendations, several important themes need to be revisited. It is often the case that a contentious relationship exists between the family and the school district. Psychologists can take a proactive approach in these cases (Ernst, Pelletier, & Simpson, 2008) by reiterating their role as including the following components: providing an assessment that will detail the child's strengths and weaknesses; reminding the members of the meeting that the psychologist performing the IEE cannot unilaterally determine eligibility for special education services, because this is the responsibility of the individualized education plan (IEP) team; and noting that a diagnosis of a condition of disability (under the Individuals With Disabilities Education Improvement Act of 2004 [IDEIA]) is also not sufficient for eligibility for special education services, that the evidence must show the child is entitled to special education services. The evidence must corroborate that demonstrated impairments are adversely affecting the child's educational functioning (in most circumstances, some of the evidence will have emerged from the collateral interviews of the school personnel within the child's educational setting). Last, the psychologist should explain that he or she is providing the school district with the information provided by the IEE but note that the school district is not obligated to follow all or any of the recommendations until the IEP incorporates the recommendations.

The final section of the feedback session (Step 8) involves a discussion of recommendations that are based on the results of the evaluation and previous discussion. The recommendations must be related to an identified need for special education services or accommodations. As stated earlier, input from the school district is critical for developing recommendations because the IEP team is responsible for the final plan. However, the psychologist can generate a list of the student's needs in the educational setting and offer concrete suggestions that are based on scientific findings and are appropriate under the special education statutes (i.e., IDEIA and Section 504 of the Rehabilitation Act of 1973). Psychologists should avoid making statements that require IEP team involvement (e.g., the child does qualify for specially designed instruction) or that prescribe a specified intervention or time of intervention (e.g., "30 minutes 2x/week of speech and language pathology services" or "The X reading program is required"). Recommendations should include what the child's needs are and what types of interventions appear appropriate; they should not indicate specific locations where interventions should occur (e.g., the resource room). For example, if a child struggles with the noise and commotion of fire drills, the evaluator could offer suggestions about how to support the child and reduce emotional and behavioral consequences following such a drill. The evaluator could include a recommendation that the child be provided a specific plan about fire drills, including where to go, whom to talk to, and how to ask for quiet time following a fire drill. In this case, the evaluator is offering this recommendation without naming specific people or locations.

Psychologist recommendations are most effective when developed with input from family and school. In fact, researchers have recently highlighted the importance of collaboration between school professionals and independent evaluators for more thorough assessments, implementable school-based recommendations, and improved academic planning (Cleary & Scott, 2011; Ernst et al., 2008; Kanne, Randolph, & Farmer, 2008). The results of the evaluation may have uncovered problems and concerns that are important to the family or the child that do not adversely affect the child's educational experience. Psychologists best serve the evaluation process by distinguishing between interventions or support that are the responsibility of the school district and those that are the responsibility of the family. Say, for example, during the course of the evaluation significant sibling discord is uncovered that is concerning to the parents. If the psychologist concludes that the difficulty between siblings is not adversely influencing the child's educational experience, he or she may recommend family or individual therapy. This would not be a recommendation involving the school and may not need to be included in a report sent to the school. It is common that parents ask about tutoring for accelerating a child's achievement beyond his or her current grade placement; this is also not something that is the responsibility of the school district. The psychologist needs to be very clear, when recommendations are made, as to who is responsible for implementing the recommendation, and she or he should explain that the findings of the evaluation show that the child's educational experience is adversely affected.

CASE EXAMPLE

At the feedback session, SW's mother was joined by her ex-husband without notifying the psychologist ahead of time. The ex-husband indicated that he had consulted with an attorney and was considering pursuing a private school placement for his son at the district's expense. This changed the initial part of the feedback meeting significantly. The psychologist recognized that he had made a mistake in not working harder to involve the father in the evaluation. The psychologist told Mr. W that he regretted not being more active in involving him in the evaluation and thanked him for coming to the feedback session. The psychologist also told Mr. W how valuable his observations would be in understanding SW. At this point, the psychologist carefully reviewed for both parents the referral information provided by the school and the concerns raised by Ms. W. The psychologist asked Mr. W to describe his experience with SW and concerns that he might have. Mr. W indicated that he was not overly concerned about his son and felt that SW was just acting like a typical boy. As the psychologist reviewed the information provided from the school and then the results from the testing, Mr. W acknowledged he did have concerns but was worried he would be blamed if he shared those concerns. By the end of the session, both parents agreed that SW should undergo a medication trial and that they would work with a psychologist to help with their parenting practices.

INDIVIDUALIZED EDUCATION PLAN MEETING

The psychologist's skill is put to the test during presentation of findings in a meeting with the family and school together (e.g., an IEP meeting). When participating in a multidisciplinary meeting, it is important to attend to a number of things, in addition to the steps described previously. These include clarifying the goals of the meeting; clarifying who will be directing the meeting and obtaining an agenda, if one has been developed; identifying who will be attending; and obtaining information regarding the scheduled length of the meeting. This information will allow psychologists to clarify their role in the meeting was well as discuss any issues regarding the time they have available to participate. The psychologist is a guest at these meetings; someone from the school district is responsible for managing time and the topics discussed. These meetings can last for 2 hours or more, and it is important to discuss which of the topics will require the psychologist's input. For example, there may be matters that do not involve the psychologist that can be addressed before or after he or she participates in the meeting.

There can be considerable tension between parents/caregivers and school staff, as well as tension between individual school staff members. Psychologists should be prepared for possible challenges to their findings, hostile responses, and nonproductive discussions between team members. Maintaining a professional demeanor is an important part of a well-developed clinical skill set. Evaluators can best serve the process by remaining dispassionate regardless of what question is asked and responding to each question with the specific information that emerged from the evaluation. Evaluators best help the team understand the psychological evidence by adhering to an educational role. Prior to the end of the meeting, or before the psychologist leaves the meeting, it is important to clarify what role, if any, the psychologist will be playing in the future.

Participation in IEP or related meetings provides an opportunity for psychologists to answer questions about any aspect of the assessment and help clarify any misunderstandings. In addition, the experience of participating in meetings with different professionals can help a psychologist better understand the various perspectives of a multidisciplinary team. With this knowledge, a psychologist will become better able to ensure that he or she provides understandable information in the future.

5

Final Report

A psychological report that integrates and summarizes the information gathered during the evaluation is integral to the independent educational evaluation (IEE). Much has been written about the purposes of the psychological report, its ethical considerations, content, language, audience, length, and inclusion of scores, as well as consideration of possible harm (Ackerman, 2006; Brooks & Iverson, 2012; Harvey, 2006; Michaels, 2006; Reynolds & Horton, 2012; Sattler & Hoge, 2006).

SECTIONS IN THE FINAL REPORT

We urge that most reports include the following 12 sections:

1. Identifying Information
2. Confidentiality Statement

http://dx.doi.org/10.1037/14318-006
Educational Evaluations of Children With Special Needs: Clinical and Forensic Considerations, by D. Breiger, K. Bishop, and G. A. H. Benjamin

3. Referral Information
4. Background/History
5. Assessment Tools/Procedures
6. Behavior Observations
7. Significant Findings
8. Impressions
9. Recommendations
10. Statement Regarding Feedback
11. Signature
12. Score Summary

1. Identifying Information

This includes the name of the examinee, date(s) of evaluation, age, grade, name of school, and clinicians involved.

2. Confidentiality Statement

This is a statement to indicate that the report contains confidential information and should be treated accordingly, for example: "HIGHLY CONFIDENTIAL: Please do not copy or distribute this information without specific permission."

3. Referral Information

The evaluator should write this section before starting the first interviews. Writing each section of the report as the evaluation process occurs will increase the accuracy of the report. We recommend that evaluators begin this process with a clear understanding of the issues and structure of the evaluation. The tasks of the evaluation will become more complicated as it progresses, and careful preparation at the start will serve the evaluator well.

The report needs to be well organized and clear. It should integrate the various sources of information in a manner that is respectful to all parties and provides a clear and accurate representation of the collected data.

4. Background/History

In this section, the evaluator reviews information that was obtained from a review of the relevant records as well as interviews with parents, teachers, the child, school district representatives, and anyone else contacted during the evaluation. Subheadings within this section include Developmental History, Medical History, Social History, and School History.

Developmental History

This section should include information regarding developmental milestones, for example, rate of acquiring language, motor, social milestones.

Medical History

Include in the Medical History section information about pertinent medical history, including the mother's pregnancy and postnatal health as well as the child's hospitalizations, significant illnesses, head trauma, developmental syndromes, medications taken, and previous medical diagnoses. Results of vision and hearing screening also should be included. Note whether the child uses glasses or a hearing aid.

Social History

This section includes a history of both the child's current social environment, for example, members of family with whom he or she lives, as well as a history of the child's development of social skills, relationships with siblings and peers, and friendships.

School History

Included in this section are details about the child's school history, including an indication of whether the child has experienced multiple school changes; school settings; attendance; current grade placement; and any specialized services, including specially designed instruction, accommodations, and modifications. Current individualized education plans (IEPs) should be reviewed in this part of the report. A review of school records—report cards, grades, behavior reports, and previous test results, including standardized assessments—should be included. The evaluator also should record in this section any teacher/school staff concerns, including areas of strength and weakness, performance on tests and daily assignments, attention, motivation, and peer relationships.

5. Assessment Tools/Procedures

This section contains a list of the names of all of the measures used in the evaluation, and all of the sources of data should be reviewed. We include the names of the people interviewed and a brief description of the written materials reviewed, for example, "May 2012 IEP from the Half-Dome School District."

6. Behavior Observations

In this section, the evaluator should describe the child's behavior during the structured and unstructured parts of the evaluation. This description typically includes information regarding the child's physical appearance, speech, language, affect/mood, observed sustained attention/concentration, activity level, motivation, and unusual behaviors/habits. The child's reactions to the assessment experience, including how the child responded to failure, success, and feedback from the examiner, is often included. For example, information about how a child responded to a challenging test item, such as an observable change in affect, decreased attention, and/or physical tic, would be helpful to include. The evaluator should conclude this section with a statement regarding his or her opinion about the reliability and validity of the results. The Behavior Observations section includes only descriptions of observable behavior, not interpretations of that behavior. Interpretations are provided in the Impressions section of the report.

7. Significant Findings

The Significant Findings section of the report should include separate paragraphs for each domain assessed (e.g., intellectual functioning, achievement, language, social). It is generally easier to understand domain-specific results rather than test-by-test results. Within each paragraph, the evaluator should summarize and integrate the significant findings. For example, for a child suspected of having an autism spectrum disorder, in the social domain the evaluator should describe all relevant assessments, highlighting the child's social strengths and challenges, and collectively summarize the findings. Organizing the data in such a way allows the reader to review the child's functioning in specific areas rather than becoming distracted by each assessment and the time-consuming task of deciphering and translating results. In addition, tests should be interpreted in context and should not be assumed to measure any factor completely (e.g., Baron, 2004).

8. Impressions

In this section, the evaluator should review and integrate the significant information reviewed in the Significant Findings section, providing a clear, succinct summary of the assessment results. No new information is discussed in this section. It is often helpful to review the referral question and provide a clear response in the initial portion of this section, for example, "Child was referred to determine if he demonstrated any learning disabilities. The results of the evaluation revealed that Child meets the diagnostic criteria for a developmental reading disorder in both fluency and comprehension."

For a child to receive special education services, he or she must have a disabling condition that is causing an adverse educational impact. The evaluator's task is to diagnose the condition and delineate the evidence as to how the diagnostic symptoms adversely affect that child's learning and school performance. Providing concrete examples of how the child's diagnosis has affected learning will increase the credibility of the report and help to establish appropriate educational plans.

In addition to a report of the child's assessment performance, this section should explore how the child relates to his or her environment. Hurewitz and Kerr (2011) noted that "the determination of educational need is inextricably linked to the educational context" (p. 9). Therefore, a child's performance in school should be evaluated not only by his or her assessment performance in an office context but also through the specific context surrounding the child's learning and behaviors. This is especially important because research has shown that evaluators often create recommendations that do not easily translate into the educational setting, limiting their utility (Kanne, Randolph, & Farmer, 2008).

9. Recommendations

The recommendations provided should initially address the referral question or questions, and any additional recommendations should follow these. We recommend prioritizing recommendations and grouping them in sequence. It is also helpful to group recommendations for similar domains of functioning together. As discussed earlier, the Individuals With Disabilities Education Improvement Act of 2004 references the need for using research-based interventions, curricula, and practices (20 U.S.C. § 1414 (b)(6)(B)). Whenever possible, recommendations should include reference research-based interventions. When recommendations are supported by peer-reviewed research they are more likely to be viewed as credible and included in academic planning (Hurewitz & Kerr, 2011).

Recommendations that are clear and consistent with education laws and allow for measurable outcomes are most credible. Recommendations should be labeled to indicate which are for the school to consider as part of specially designed instruction and which are covered by Section 504 of the Rehabilitation Act of 1973. Recommendations for a particular classroom, teacher-to-student ratio, a specific school, or specific hours of intervention should not be provided. The evaluator's goal is to describe the child's disabilities and needs and provide general suggestions for intervention. Although it is the role of the IEP team to determine where and how the interventions will be provided, the evaluator can greatly assist this process by providing a report in which each recommendation is related to the assessment findings and that shows how each recommendation is intended to support the child. For example, it is not enough to simply recommend that a child be given a preferential setting or front-row seating. This is a common general recommendation seen in reports, and it is provided for various reasons. Including the reasoning for the recommendation allows readers to see why it would be helpful and not simply view it as an arbitrary suggestion. This clarity is likely to increase the application and inclusion of the evaluator's recommendations within the IEP. Other recommendations that may be the responsibility of the family, not the school, also may be listed.

10. Statement Regarding Feedback

A statement documenting the date of feedback meetings as well as who participated in the meetings is provided in this section of the report.

11. Signature

This section contains the evaluator's name, professional title, degree, and contact information.

12. Score Summary

It is common to include a separate Score Summary that provides, in tabular form, the scores from the evaluation. It is helpful to provide footnotes to explain the range of scores that fall within the average range, for example, "Scores between 90 and 110 are considered to be within the average range, scores below 85 are considered to be below average, and scores above 115 are considered to be above average."

CONCLUSION

The provision of feedback and the written report are the culmination of the evaluation process. Interpretation of the results is a complex process that requires the psychologist to be familiar with a large number of important concepts—for example, assessing the reliability and validity of the measures used; diagnostic criteria of a large number of childhood mental and medical disorders; and statistical concepts, such as interpreting change (e.g., Sherman & Brooks, 2012). We have found that the process outlined in this chapter increases the likelihood that families and school district personnel understand the results and recommendations of the evaluation. This fosters the development of appropriate and helpful interventions and accommodations that can be developed in a collaborative environment.

For an example of a complete independent educational evaluation report, see Appendix A.

6

Presentation in Due Process Hearings and Postruling Interactions

A special education due process hearing is one of three administrative remedies available to parents and school districts under the Individuals With Disabilities Education Improvement Act of 2004 and Section 504 of the Rehabilitation Act of 1973 to resolve disputes between parents and schools regarding children with disabilities. The other two are (a) mediation and (b) appeals to a state or federal court. By the time a case reaches the due process stage there typically would have been attempts at other remedies proposed by either the family or the school. In some cases, however, the attorney for the family is intent from the beginning on bringing the case to a due process hearing in order to obtain financial penalties from the school district to pay for outcomes such as private school placement or specific interventions.

Following the guidelines in this book will lessen the chances that psychologists will find themselves testifying in a special education due process

http://dx.doi.org/10.1037/14318-007
Educational Evaluations of Children With Special Needs: Clinical and Forensic Considerations, by D. Breiger, K. Bishop, and G. A. H. Benjamin

hearing. However, a variety of reasons that do not have to do with the quality of an independent educational evaluation lead families or schools to turn to a due process hearing. For example, parents might believe that the individualized education plan (IEP) was not appropriate or was not implemented appropriately, that the child was denied free appropriate public education, that the child is not making appropriate academic progress in areas covered by IEP, that the evaluation for eligibility was flawed, or that the school is unable to provide an appropriate educational program.

WHAT HAPPENS IN A DUE PROCESS HEARING?

A due process hearing is conducted much like a court trial. It is a litigation process that is formal and adversarial. It usually involves expert witnesses on both sides and can generate considerable hostility and bitterness. In a typical due process hearing, the parents and the school district are each represented by an attorney. The procedures for a due process hearing may vary according the state's specific laws. Similar to other court trials, each side presents its case by submitting evidence, examining witnesses (each party can subpoena witnesses), and preparing briefs. The trial often lasts for many days and is stressful for most of the people involved. The Impartial Hearing Officer (IHO, often a judge) listens to the testimony and issues a formal decision based on case law. The formal decision is conveyed to both parties in writing. The IHO's rulings depend on who brought the case to the due processing hearing and what that party requested. For example, the IHO might rule that the IEP was inappropriate and require that the school district provide a requested intervention as well as pay the family's attorney fees. Some rulings can involve significant amounts of money, for example, requiring the school district to pay for a private school in another state. Frequently, the IHO may find that the district made some mistakes but that those mistakes did not deny the child free appropriate public education and agree that the school district's evaluation and IEP were appropriate.

Many people find the prospect of testifying in court to be daunting; however, this need not be the case. The straightforward approach we outline in this chapter provides a helpful guide for psychologists who must participate in a due process hearing as an expert witness. In addition, we encourage psychologists to gain a richer understanding of being an expert witness by reading other books that offer case examples and discuss common scenarios and forensic issues (e.g., Brodsky, 2012; Sherman & Brooks, 2012).

HOW TO PREPARE AND ACT AS AN EXPERT WITNESS DURING A DUE PROCESS HEARING

It is advisable for the evaluator to reread the entire evaluation report before the day of trial testimony. This will ensure that the report and findings are fresh in the evaluator's mind and that he or she will thereby be better able to field questions.

Preparing for the Hearing

In preparing for testimony, the evaluator should consider how to remain uninfluenced by the situational demands that can lead to the evaluator being viewed as simply another one-sided advocate. In particular, the evaluator can best serve the process by remaining dispassionate; maintaining a steady demeanor, no matter what question is asked; and responding to the question with the specific information that emerged from the evaluation. The evaluator can best help the judge understand the psychological evidence by adhering to an educational role. The evaluator's demeanor should remain professional and matter-of-fact throughout testimony.

Giving Testimony and Responding to Questions

Testimony at the hearing will begin with the employing counsel establishing the evaluator's qualifications as an expert witness on direct examination. The attorney will ask for a full description of the evaluator's academic degrees, evidence of specialization, current duties of employment, honors, number and content of publications, and previous practical applications of expertise. However, no particular set of criteria exists to establish whether an expert is qualified to provide testimony about special education cases. In general, qualification occurs without difficulty because the expert's credentials were accepted at the onset of the evaluation.

If qualification becomes an issue, the opposing counsel will object that the expert is not qualified and cannot state an opinion. Trial strategy dictates inflicting damage on the credibility of the witness as soon as possible. The opposing counsel will ask the court to conduct a *voir dire* (a preliminary examination to determine the competency of an expert or other witness) with an evaluator before proceeding in an attempt to persuade the judge that the person is not an expert. Even if the judge qualifies the evaluator, the opposing counsel may focus on the supposed inadequacy of the evaluator's credentials or lack of experience in conducting special education evaluations, to dampen the effect of the evaluator's direct testimony.

Direct examination continues after the evaluator is qualified as an expert. The employing attorney asks open-ended questions to enable the evaluator to convey opinions and the rationale behind them. The employing attorney must not ask leading questions. The evaluator should discuss in advance with the employing attorney how the testimony will unfold; the approach used during the meeting with the family and school personnel (see Chapter 4, this volume) can be used again during this part of the process.

Until a direct question is asked of the evaluator, she or he must remain silent. Often, the attorneys will begin to address each other or make statements about the report. To maintain the role of an educator, the evaluator should remain detached from this type of attorney interaction.

Finally, an attorney will ask the evaluator a direct question. If applicable, the following suggestions will help the evaluator educate the attorneys during the responses and avoid raising doubts about the evaluator's credibility or knowledge (Bennett, Bryant, VandenBos, & Greenwood, 1990; Luvera, 1981; Pappas, 1987; Watson, 1978):

- Answer questions directly and concisely, without volunteering unsolicited information. If a yes or no will suffice, say no more, but if an answer requires qualification, you are not compelled to give more than a simple response.

- Respond to understandable questions only: Paraphrasing a confusing question may suggest an entirely different matter unrelated to the attorney's inquiry. If you are unclear as to what the lawyer is asking, request that he or she state the question differently.

- Draw reasonable inferences between the data of the case and your expert knowledge: This type of opinion-based evidence relies on reasonable psychological probability and is not subject to the stringent demands of scientific validity or reliability.

- Use plain language: Explain all technical terms, so that a lay audience would understand. Also, avoid using extreme adjectives or superlatives.

- Refrain from stating that any single article or text is authoritative or you will be viewed as having relied explicitly on the article or text to formulate opinions. Opposing counsel may use any part of such an article or text to impeach your credibility then or later during discovery (described below) or during the due process hearing.

Attorneys may seek to test the evaluator's credibility by using any of the following strategies. First, one of the attorneys (usually the attorney who perceives that her or his client has fared worse) may skip from one subject to the next in attempt to keep the evaluator off balance. To handle this, evaluators should keep the points above in mind as they give responses. The evaluator can also slow attorneys down by having them point out the specific area of the report to which they are referring or by asking them to provide a broader reiteration of the question. Second, attorneys may summarize the evaluator's findings inaccurately, using connotative words or shading the wording to their advantage (e.g., "So, doctor, you say here that the other party *hesitated* to answer some of your questions; what explains that kind of arrogance?"). The evaluator should correct any deliberate misconstruals and address the question at hand specifically by listing each measure that led to the corroboration of the particular finding under discussion. Attention to detail and the meaning of words is critical (given that many terms have independent legal significance apparent only to attorneys). Third, an attorney may ask compound questions that assume facts not raised by either party during the pendency of the evaluation. The evaluator must separate the unproven assumptions to avoid the taint of speculation and simply state that neither party—despite many opportunities to do so—raised the issue during the evaluation. Fourth, attorneys may press the evaluator to specify a time frame (e.g., how long the child will require special education services). Questions involving a period of time are particularly difficult, and any answer should be labeled as an estimate. For example, in regard to how long the child will require special education services, too many intervening factors would prevent anything but an estimate.

Parsimonious testimony will help keep the judge focused on the issues. If the evaluator can establish eye contact with the judge and the judge seems comfortable with such contact, this may help to keep the judge's attention. The evaluator should testify in plain language, avoiding technical terms, assumptions not supported by an earlier foundation, and concepts that assume the judge's knowledge of the evaluation report. All opinions must be supported with full descriptions of the data, the techniques used to gather the data, and the inferences drawn from the corroborating measures. In addition, the evaluator should identify all vulnerable portions of the assessment process or analyses of the results. For instance, a test that has poor psychometric properties might have been used in an evaluation for a hypothesis-generating purpose. In this case, the evaluator would qualify its use by speaking about the test results' lack of reliability absent further corroboration from other measures or parts of the evaluation process. The testimony should remain consistent with the evaluation report, interrogatory responses, or deposition statements.

After direct examination is finished, the opposing counsel will begin cross-examination. The evaluator will often be limited to responding yes or no to the leading questions of the opposing counsel. In this respect, testifying during cross-examination might appear easier than during direct examination. However, the opposing counsel will attempt to discredit the evaluator and the evaluator's findings by using tactics described earlier. A typical attack on the evaluator's credibility will occur as the opposing counsel asks leading questions about the lack of independence of the evaluator or the thoroughness of the evaluation process. The opposing counsel may allege that financial considerations have biased the evaluator. Following the procedures described in Chapter 3 about outlining one's fees ahead of time will help defend against this type of attack.

Another typical attempt to question the evaluator's thoroughness occurs when the opposing counsel cites inconsistent testimony. The opposing counsel often presents examples of inconsistent testimony unfairly. If the cross-examiner reads from an interrogatory or deposition transcript to show the inconsistency, the material often is taken out of context. Certainly the evaluator can ask to review the document or deposition transcript before responding to the cross-examination question. If the matter has been taken out context, the evaluator can state as much. Such a remark might lead the employing attorney to make an objection if the opposing attorney attempts to close off any elaboration by insisting that the evaluator simply answer the leading question with a yes or no.

Yet another typical method by which the opposing counsel attempts to impeach the expert's credibility is to claim a lack of foundation for the evaluator's opinion. The opposing counsel may challenge the evaluator's thoroughness by questioning whether he or she omitted certain facts or relied on the wrong facts to form opinions. In response, the evaluator can point out, for instance, that during the feedback interviews the party had a further opportunity to contest each of the findings and can explain why multiple measures led to the corroborated findings. Judges are impressed with such thoroughness and attempts to maintain a fair process.

Leading questions can be irritating because they attempt to paint a black-and-white picture while leaving little room for accurate explanations. Often, the opposing counsel intends to increase the frustration level of the evaluator and perhaps even provoke an outburst that would compromise the evaluator's professional demeanor. When the opposing counsel allows the evaluator to provide a fuller explanation about a particular issue, the purpose is to lead the evaluator away from the basic facts of the case and give full rein to the expert's pride and wordiness in the hope of possibly placing her or him in a bad light. Behaving as an educator and as an objective professional can be difficult when being grilled and set up by a good cross-examiner. The best course is to avoid arguing or appearing as a staunch advocate. Instead, the evaluator should remain polite and cooperative and answer all the questions directly and dispassionately.

At the end of the cross-examination, the employing attorney will conduct a redirect examination. Once again, the questions will be open-ended and provide the evaluator an opportunity to explain points raised during the cross-examination that may have been misleading or have left an incomplete impression because of the expert's brief and simple responses. Often, a recess will be declared before redirect examination begins. The employing attorney may have suggestions about what points raised during the earlier cross-examination require clarification or emphasis.

MEETING WITH A PARTY WHO REQUESTS MORE INFORMATION AFTER A RULING HAS BEEN ISSUED

Sometimes a party will want additional time to meet with the evaluator after the IHO has issued a ruling. We recommend that the evaluator consider such a meeting for two reasons. First, a party can gain closure about the evaluation process in such a meeting, and this closure reduces the risk that a complaint will be filed. Second, the party can gain additional information about the evaluation findings that may help that party understand how to better assist the child. However, in special education cases, if a due process decision is appealed, the court has discretion to allow or require additional factual testimony. Therefore, the evaluator should avoid any interaction with an adverse party unless agreed to by the hiring attorney/party or unless additional depositions/discovery require divulgence of additional testimony.

In most such meetings, the party will raise concerns about evidence that, in her or his view, the evaluator disregarded. The evaluator should matter-of-factly review the evaluation process and remind the party that opportunities arose during the evaluation process to correct the record or provide additional evidence. The evaluator should continue to discuss the findings as they are presented in the evaluation report.

Evaluators who are required to take part as expert witnesses in due process hearings should not be intimidated. Careful preparation and knowledge of what may or may not happen, which we have provided in this chapter, can ease the process considerably.

Afterword

In this book, we set out to describe a step-by-step evaluation protocol for generating comprehensive educational evaluations. The approach we have described is grounded in clinical research as well as many years of experience with a large variety of cases. It also is congruent with the current ethical standards developed by the American Psychological Association (see http://www.apa.org/ethics/code/index.aspx).

In the initial chapters, we provided information to help readers understand the context of independent education evaluations, as well as the laws and requirements that will shape the organization of a psychologist's evaluation findings and final report. In the remaining chapters, we presented a detailed step-by-step approach to conducting an independent education evaluation. Beginning with the initial referral, we covered how to prepare for the initial interview, issues of confidentiality, the importance of documentation, careful and ethical data collection, and ways to ensure transparency and minimize bias. Our framework uses an approach that seeks to minimize errors in clinical judgment by emphasizing converging evidence and using a cautious approach in reaching conclusions and interpretations. A major focus of this protocol is how to provide an atmosphere in which feedback can be provided in a way that is clear and reduces misunderstandings. The written report that summarizes the evaluation is a tool that documents the care the evaluator took to be objective; it serves to answer the referral question and provide useful recommendations that meet the standards of the laws. Involvement in legal proceedings, such as due process hearings, is an unavoidable aspect of this type of work. By organizing the psychological evidence in a way that relates to the pertinent legal standards, and striving to maintain an objective point of view, the evaluator can be prepared for the challenges in adversarial situations.

We believe that conducting educational evaluations in the manner we have described will serve and protect the best interests of the child. We strongly encourage evaluators to continue to review new and evolving information regarding clinical, legal, and ethical standards. We hope that in this book we have provided information that will help clinicians conduct effective evaluations that help improve the lives and children and their families.

Appendix A
Sample Independent Educational Evaluation Report

The following is a sample report that demonstrates the recommended format for an independent educational evaluation. The report is based on a composite of cases we have actually evaluated. The identities of the parties discussed herein have been masked so that no particular fact pattern would lead to a breach of confidentiality.

NEUROPSYCHOLOGICAL EVALUATION SUMMARY

Client name:	SW
Date of visit (last contact):	September 10, 2010
Age:	10 years, 7 months
Grade:	Grade 5
Referral:	Royal Coachman District

HIGHLY CONFIDENTIAL

Please do not copy or distribute this information without specific permission.

REFERRAL INFORMATION

SW is a 10-year-, 7-month-old male who was referred for this evaluation by the Royal Coachman School District to gain a more comprehensive understanding of his executive and social/emotional functioning to assist with appropriate educational planning, programming, and placement as well as to offer suggestions for resources/recommendations for parents. Detailed information on SW's development, medical, educational, social, and family history was gathered during the current evaluation. Only that which is relevant to referral questions as stated above is reported here.

EVALUATION INFORMATION

SW was evaluated on September 10, 2010, by a team composed of Mr. P, psychometrist, and GM, PhD, neuropsychologist and clinic director. In addition to neuropsychological tests and past records (as listed in the assessment procedures), information was obtained from the following:

08/25/2010: Semistructured interview with SW's mother
09/08/2010: Interview with SW's pediatrician, Dr. P, MD
08/30/2010: Interview with SW's psychotherapist
08/31/2010: Interview with individuals at the Royal Coachman School District, including SW's school psychologist, Ms. A; third grade teacher, Ms. B; and special education teacher/individualized education plan [IEP] case worker, Ms. C.

PRESENT CONCERNS

According to Ms. A, school psychologist; Ms. B, third grade teacher; and Ms. C, special education teacher/IEP case manager, at Rainbow Elementary School, the school is primarily concerned about SW's significant difficulties with attention and impulsivity, which are severely affecting his academic, psychological, and social functioning. They are also concerned with the emergence of other concerning behaviors since winter of last year, including lying, manipulation, stealing, and externalizing (oppositional and defiant actions, violations of others) and internalizing (depressed mood, statements indicating suicidal ideation) behaviors. Secondary concerns pertain to SW's learning and academic difficulties. Ms. A reported that throughout the course of the last several months of the past school year, SW was also exhibiting significant difficulties with organization, executive functioning, inattention, and impulsivity. Of considerable concern were several instances in which SW inappropriately touched other students (e.g., grabbed their body parts in inappropriate areas, hugging, squeezing) and violated their privacy (e.g., stared at them under bathroom stalls), which were reported to the school principal by concerned parents.

According to SW's mother, Ms. W, she also is concerned about the difficulties noted by SW's school regarding the increasing behavioral, social, academic, and learning difficulties, as well as verbal statements indicating suicidal ideation and anxiety pertaining to school. Ms. W expressed concerned about SW returning to Rainbow Elementary School because of his difficulties experienced there in the last several months of the school year.

Ms. W suggested that attention-deficit/hyperactivity disorder (ADHD), sensory processing disorder, and dyslexia be considered during the neurocognitive assessment. Both in the home and school contexts, SW was reported to demonstrate difficulties remembering information and following through with directions and requests made by others, particularly when they involve multiple steps.

Ms. W reported that SW has increasingly shown improvements in anxiety and social functioning since school ended in June. However, SW continued to exhibit anxious behaviors when he was reminded about school. Although Ms. W was initially reluctant to send SW back to Rainbow Elementary School at the beginning of this school year, SW attended the first week of school, and no issues were reported.

MEDICAL AND DEVELOPMENTAL HISTORIES

Medical and developmental histories were obtained through parent report by Ms. W. No significant issues during the prenatal or perinatal periods were reported. SW was born full-term and was delivered normally without signs of fetal distress. SW did not experience any medical difficulties during infancy. Ms. W described SW as an "easy," sociable baby who was very active in the toddler years.

SW met all developmental milestones on time with the exception of his speech; he did not produce understandable sentences until he was approximately 3 years old. He was toilet trained at 3 (bladder control) and 4 (bowel control) years of age. SW continues to have episodes of bed-wetting at night (nocturnal enuresis), which were more frequent at the end of the previous school year. Although gross motor skills were are not an area of parental concern, SW exhibits considerable difficulty with fine motor skills. He recently learned to tie his shoes at age 9.

No hearing, vision, or chronic health issues were reported. SW has never been hospitalized. No history of head injuries, concussions, or seizures was reported.

EDUCATIONAL HISTORY

SW recently began fourth grade at Rainbow Elementary School. He has been receiving an IEP and intensive services since he qualified for special services under the category of "Developmental Delay" in April 2007. He currently receives an IEP under the category of "Learning Disabilities" following additional educational testing in February 2009. His most recent IEP is dated 09/01/2010. The IEP indicates that SW receives specialized instruction from a special education teacher throughout the day in reading (comprehension and fluency), writing, math problem solving, organization and executive functioning, behavior, and oral expression. He receives speech and language therapy from a speech and language pathologist for 30 minutes a week as well as occupational therapy from an occupational therapist for 15 minutes biweekly. Finally, SW is also part of a social skills class that follows Michelle Garcia-Winner's curriculum to address social interaction difficulties.

Ms. W reported that she had suspected learning difficulties since SW was 3 years of age because of his lack of progression in skill development in the areas of language, communications, reading, and writing. SW has not been expelled from school; however, recent complaints have been made to his school principal by parents of his peers regarding inappropriate touching of other students as well as violations of other's privacy in bathrooms.

PREVIOUS EVALUATION RESULTS

In June 2007, SW received educational testing through the Royal Coachman School District. In summary, the results revealed low average overall cognitive ability, verbal comprehension, and processing speed abilities, as well as average (age-appropriate) working memory and nonverbal/perceptual reasoning abilities as assessed by the WISC–IV. Overall, SW's academic skills were within the borderline range, and oral language skills were in the average range. SW's overall adaptive functioning was between the below-average and borderline ranges. Difficulties with sensory processing were also reported.

In February 2010, SW once again received educational testing through the Royal Coachman School District to determine eligibility for special services under a different category than developmental delay and to obtain his current level of functioning by his ninth birthday. The results of this recent assessment revealed verbal skills in the borderline range and nonverbal skills in the low average range. SW's spatial and working memory abilities were in the average range, as assessed by the DAS–2. Overall, SW's academic skills were variable; oral language, listening comprehension, early reading skills, and paper-and-pencil math skills (numerical operations) were in the average range. Written expression was in the low average range. Basic reading skills, oral math problem solving, sentence combining, and math fluency were in the borderline range. SW's reading comprehension and oral reading fluency were in the very impaired range. SW's communication skills, as assessed by a speech and language pathologist, fell in the below-average range. SW's fine and perceptual motor skills were average; however, relative sensory processing difficulties were once again noted. Finally, significant issues with interpersonal relationships, learning problems, inappropriate behaviors, internalizing and externalizing (defiance, inattention, hyperactivity, etc.) behaviors, and executive functioning were also found on the basis of both the parent and teacher reports.

The results of this recent testing through the Royal Coachman School District indicated that SW met criteria for learning disabilities that were deemed to significantly affect his performance in all academic areas, executive functioning, and behavior within the classroom environment. At this time, it was recommended that SW receive an IEP in oral reading fluency, reading and comprehension, basic reading, written expression, math reasoning/problem solving, organization/executive functioning and behavior under the category of specific learning disabilities.

SOCIAL/EMOTIONAL/PSYCHOLOGICAL HISTORY

SW lives with his mother. He does not have siblings. SW's father has not lived in the family home consistently since 2007, when he and Ms. W initially separated. Ms. W and SW's father's divorce was recently finalized. Issues with SW's mood, anxiety, and behavior were observed to increase from the period of SW's parents' most recent separation and divorce (April 2009) to the present time.

Ms. W and SW's teachers reported significant concerns about SW's current behavioral difficulties both within and outside the home. Within the home, SW often argues with adults, actively defies or refuses to comply with his mother's requests or rules, and often deliberately does things to annoy other people. He is noted to be particularly aggressive with his mother and has on several occasions hit her (e.g., on one occasion while she was driving) as well as other family members. He has broken things when angry and behaves with anger and resentfulness when he is frustrated. These behavioral difficulties have been observed since he was a toddler and appear to be triggered when he is anxious, under pressure or time constraints, experiencing stress or difficulties making decisions, or when he has done something wrong. Ms. W also reported that SW has been caught shoplifting twice in the past few weeks; his teachers have also observed stealing within the school. SW has exhibited a pattern of lying and denying responsibility for actions in home and school contexts. At times, these behaviors appeared to be a result of sequencing and memory difficulties; however, at other times teachers reported that these behaviors were intentional given that SW later accepted responsibility when he could not deny responsibility.

SW was diagnosed with ADHD, combined subtype, by his pediatrician, Dr. P, in January 2010. Significant difficulties with attention, hyperactivity, impulsivity, planning and organization, and fidgeting were also reported by Ms. W and the school. At the time of receiving this diagnosis, Dr. P recommended a trial of Adderall XR 10 mg; however, he reported that Ms. W was reluctant because of her preference for naturalistic approaches to wellness as well as a family history of substance abuse and dependence. After receiving this diagnosis, SW saw a naturopath who recommended taking folate supplements and suggested that he had a genetic mutation contributing to depletion of folate in his system. Ms. W reported improvement in self-awareness and improvement in memory and hyperactivity since SW started taking folate supplements; however, improvements were not noted by SW's teachers or Dr. P. Dr. P prescribed Concerta 18 mg after Ms. W reported a concerning escalation in behavioral and emotional difficulties. After SW had been taking Concerta for 2 weeks, Dr. P prescribed an increased dose of 36 mg. Ms. W reported that within 2 days of taking this higher dose, she observed an increase in SW's behavioral and sleep difficulties as well as appetite suppression. She also expressed concern about similarities between SW's behavior and behaviors of individuals with substance abuse problems. Ms. W discontinued this medication after a few days. Dr. P has not seen SW since that time. Currently, SW is taking folate supplements to manage his ADHD symptoms. SW's teachers report that his attention and impulsivity difficulties are the most severe of any child within the school and have thus far been resistant to behavioral intervention.

When difficulties at school arose at the end of the school year, SW reported suicidal ideation to his mother on several occasions. At this time, he also exhibited depressed mood and anhedonia (e.g., not wanting to go outside or sing). This persisted for a few months. He exhibited similar mood difficulties during the period of his parents' most recent separation. However, Ms. W reported that SW is not exhibiting difficulties with mood at this time and has shown improvement in this area since the end of the previous school year.

Per parent report, SW exhibits some symptoms of generalized anxiety, particularly pertaining to school and his father's well-being. SW expresses worries with the theme of abandonment, particularly by his parents. He appears preoccupied by worries pertaining to his body, particularly blood, and is anxious about his social status. Ms. W reported that toward the end of the school year, SW reported significant somatic complaints in the mornings before school and exhibited some mild school refusal, which did not result in significant school absence. When anxious, SW often seeks reassurance from his mother. His teachers typically do not observe anxious behaviors. SW's psychotherapist, Ms. F, whom he has been seeing on a weekly basis since January 2009, initially diagnosed him with anxiety disorder, not otherwise specified. She reported on 09/20/2010 that she considers the disorder to currently be in remission. In their sessions together, Ms. F reported that she has been teaching him social and self-regulation skills.

No history of physical or sexual abuse was reported. Per parent report, SW has witnessed verbal aggression and conflict between his parents on numerous occasions. Ms. W reported there is a family history of external-izing (ADHD) and internalizing (anxiety, depression) disorders, learning disorders, narcissistic personality disorder, substance abuse, and trauma.

According to Ms. W and the school, SW has significant difficulties forming and maintaining friendships. According to Ms. W and SW, SW's peers avoid him at school and tell him that he is mean and a bully. When Ms. W addressed incidents of inappropriate touching and violations of others, SW denied engaging in these behaviors and reported that he did not remember doing this. He also engaged in head banging when his mother brought the issue up in conversation. SW spends time with family mem-bers who are either older or much younger than he. Ms. W reported that he has been observed to be physically aggressive toward them on occasion.

No issues with stereotyped behaviors, tics, obsessions and compul-sions, hallucinations, or delusions were reported.

ASSESSMENT PROCEDURES

- Wechsler Intelligence Scale for Children, Fourth Edition, selected subtests
- Wechsler Abbreviated Scale of Intelligence—Second Edition
- Test of Memory Malingering
- Test of Word Reading Efficiency, Second Edition
- Qualitative Reading Inventory—5
- Receptive One-Word Picture Vocabulary Test—4th
- Grooved pegboard
- NEPSY–II (A Developmental NEuroPSYchological Assessment), Sec-ond Edition, selected subtests
- Wide Range Assessment of Memory and Learning, selected subtests

- Wide Range Assessment of Memory and Learning—2, selected subtests
- Symbol Digit Modalities Test
- Adaptive Behavior Assessment System—Second Edition
- Behavioral Assessment System for Children—Second Edition
- Behavior Rating Inventory of Executive Function
- Semistructured clinical interviews
- Previous IEP reports and school evaluations

BEHAVIORAL OBSERVATIONS

SW presented to the evaluation as a 10-year-old who appeared to be his age. He was appropriately groomed and dressed for the evaluation. SW's speech was clear and coherent; however, it was at times tangential in content. His affect was broad ranged, and his mood was appropriate. On several occasions, the examiner needed to redirect his attention back to task/subject at hand. SW was very fidgety in his chair and frequently needed reminders to listen carefully. However, he was able to refocus with prompting from the examiner. SW was pleasant and cooperative and never complained, even when completing activities that were obviously very difficult for him (e.g., reading tasks). SW appeared motivated to do his best on the tasks presented. Effort level/motivation was evaluated using a standardized assessment measure, and there were no concerns in this area. The following results are considered to be an accurate reflection of his current level of functioning.

SIGNIFICANT FINDINGS

Intellectual Functioning

SW's overall cognitive abilities are difficult to summarize in one score because of the significant difference between his verbal and nonverbal/ perceptual reasoning abilities. SW's verbal comprehension abilities are in the below average range and in the 5th percentile, meaning that SW performed more poorly than 95% of other children his age on this assessment measure. SW's nonverbal/perceptual reasoning abilities are in the

average range (50th percentile). These scores suggest that SW has considerably more difficulty understanding verbal information and expressing
his understanding through language as compared with many of his peers.
Conversely, on visual tasks that do not require expressive language, SW
solved novel problems and synthesized information from several sources
at an age-appropriate level.

Academic Achievement

On standardized tests of academic achievement, SW demonstrated below-
average efficiency (< 1st percentile) of individual word decoding (reading sight words) and phonetic decoding (sounding out unfamiliar words;
2nd percentile).

SW read passages of materials at significantly below age-appropriate
reading speed. At the Grade 1 level, he read approximately 14 words per
minute; at the primer level, he read approximately 11 words per minute.
When asked to retell the story without the materials to reference, he had
difficulty recalling the details of the story. Without being able to reference
the material, SW's comprehension of first-grade–level materials was at the
frustration level. His comprehension of primer-grade–level materials was
at the instructional level.

1. The *independent level* is the level at which the student can read without assistance.
2. The *instructional level* is the level at which the material is challenging
   for the student: neither too difficult nor too easy.
3. The *frustration level* is the level at which the student would find it
   frustrating to try to understand what he or she reads.

Language and Psycholinguistic Skills

SW was given a measure that examined his verbal fluency, or the ability
to rapidly name words belonging to a semantic or phonemic category.
Verbal fluency taps lexical knowledge and semantic memory organization. SW's rapid retrieval of verbal information was in the average to

low-average range. This indicates that SW is likely able to access his word knowledge within age-expected levels.

Although SW's single-word receptive vocabulary, or understanding of words spoken to him, was above average (79th percentile), his ability to process and execute oral instructions of increasing syntactic complexity was in the below-average range (5th percentile).

Sensory–Perceptual and Perceptual–Motor Function

SW's fine motor speed and coordination were in the average range in his preferred (right) hand and in the low average range in his nonpreferred (left) hand.

Learning and Recall

Overall, SW performed in the below-average range on measures of learning and memory recall of verbal and visual information; however, there was variability in his individual subscale scores. He performed better when asked to immediately recall details from a story that was read to him. Although he was unable to recall many details of the story on his own after a delay, he was able to recognize information when he was asked questions in yes/no format. This suggests that SW benefits from learning information presented to him in a narrative context and that he is better able to remember information when given prompts and cues. SW's ability to learn verbal information was below average; however, he benefited from repetition and practice, which resulted in improvements in his performance. SW also performed at an age-appropriate level on a visual memory task.

Information-Processing Speed

SW performed below age-appropriate levels on visual tasks requiring speed of processing and the ability to sustain attention and inhibit impulsive responding.

Executive-Control Processes

Overall, SW demonstrated below age-appropriate ability to hold information in short-term memory and apply it to the current task (i.e., working memory).

SW had difficulty shifting his attention appropriately and demonstrated below age-appropriate ability controlling impulsive responses on a complex task.

Social and Emotional Functioning

SW's ability to recognize emotions on photographs of children's faces was age appropriate. However, he demonstrated below-average ability in attributing mental states—beliefs, intentions, thoughts, emotions, pretending—to himself and others and in understanding that others have beliefs, desires, and intentions that are different from his own.

Standardized questionnaires completed by Ms. W indicated that SW demonstrated significantly elevated levels of attention problems (including hyperactivity and inattention), conduct problems, externalizing and internalizing problems, depression, somatization, atypicality, withdrawal, and functional communication difficulties. Significant concerns were also noted in the areas of anger and emotional self-control, social skills and communication, and negative emotionality. SW was described as having delays in all areas of adaptive behaviors, particularly in the area of functional academics.

IMPRESSIONS

SW is a 10-year-old male who was referred for neuropsychological evaluation by the Royal Coachman School District because of a history of significant difficulties with attention and impulsivity and the recent increase in oppositional and defiant behaviors as well as internalizing symptoms. Integrating findings from Ms. W, the school, pediatrician, and psychotherapist as well as our behavioral observations and the results of standardized testing indicate that SW has ADHD, combined subtype and meets criteria for oppositional defiant disorder (ODD).

SW's symptoms of ADHD are severely affecting his academic, psychological, and social functioning and are likely exacerbating his oppositional/defiant behaviors, including the unusual and inappropriate touching. This is especially concerning in light of research showing that children, like SW, who have ADHD, ODD, and learning disabilities are at significant risk for following a trajectory of antisocial behavior into adulthood, including substance abuse and dependency, forensic/police involvement, academic failure, and a range of psychological difficulties. As such, it is critical that SW receives the appropriate evidence-based intervention not only in school but also in the home; formal parent behavioral training needs to complement behavioral interventions in order for treatment to be effective and generalize across contexts.

The results of this neuropsychological evaluation are largely consistent with educational evaluations that SW has completed in the past. SW's nonverbal and perceptual abilities are age appropriate; however, his verbal, oral language, and reading skills are far below his same-age peers. Although SW's single-word receptive vocabulary is well developed, he struggles when required to think abstractly and express himself using words. He also shows core deficits in phonological processing skills. As such, his difficulties in this area are consistent with a diagnosis of a reading disorder (dyslexia), which results in an adverse impact on his academic performance in all areas. SW also showed considerable variability in his performance on tasks assessing the same skill area (e.g., learning and memory), which is consistent with a diagnosis of ADHD. His severe difficulties with attention and impulsivity are affecting his academic and skill performance. These attention difficulties are also likely contributing to his poor adaptive functioning.

At this time, SW does not meet criteria for a mood or anxiety disorder; however, his emotional functioning is clearly negatively affected by family conflict and closely connected to his parents' marital conflict and patterns of interaction. Ms. W reported that SW has anxiety pertaining to school; as such, it important for the school and Ms. W to monitor this. Finally, SW's difficulties taking the perspective of others may in part be contributing to his difficulties in peer relationships.

RECOMMENDATIONS

In light of the background information and evaluation, the following recommendations are made. It is hoped that these recommendations will
serve as a guide to SW's IEP team in developing strategies and identifying
resources to best meet his individual needs. We would advise SW's IEP
team to review the information from this evaluation and the proposed
recommendations in order to develop an IEP and determine which services and accommodations would best meet his needs.

Recommendations for the School

Specialized Instruction

- We recommend that SW continue to qualify for specialized instruction
  and Section 504 accommodations and that the emphasis be on curricula that SW can effectively master, so that he can experience success
  in the academic context.
- We recommend that SW's academic programming reflect his current
  level of skill development and knowledge. Given SW's communication
  and reading difficulties, instructions should be read to him, and the
  focus should be on capturing his performance with the use of rewards
  and positive feedback.
- Instructions should be specific and direct, accompanied by visual supports and repeated several times, and should not exceed the amount of
  information he is able to keep track of.
- SW performs better when he is asked to recognize information (e.g.,
  using a multiple-choice format) versus recall information on his own.
  As such, this type of testing will likely result in a performance that more
  accurately reflects his knowledge.

Behavior

- We recommend that SW receive behavior management to address
  his ODD and ADHD in both home (i.e., with parents) and school
  contexts. This intervention should focus on positive feedback and
  rewards.

- Given that problematic incidents at school have tended to occur during bathroom breaks and recess, these periods should be highly structured and supervised.
- We recommend that formal functional behavior analyses be conducted in multiple environments at school (e.g., classroom, recess), to further delineate the antecedents of SW's disruptive behavior and inform treatment targets.
- The school has been very responsive to SW's difficulties and has been implementing interventions to help. Some additional specific suggestions for managing SW's behavior include the following:
  - Use a prearranged, unintrusive, nonpunitive signal, such as a tap on the shoulder, as a means of bringing SW back on task when he drifts off.
  - Minimize background noise in any classroom or study situation as much as possible.
  - Break down large assignments into a series of smaller units.
  - Use an activity-based approach (e.g., responding to questions, working with peers, hands-on work). Ideally, SW would be actively engaged in a series of short activities with frequent feedback about his performance.
  - Add novelty to tasks, especially toward the end of tasks, to keep SW interested. Eliminate repetition within tasks as much as possible.
  - Minimize complex verbal communication and augment simple verbal instructions with the use of gestures, pictures, or charts. We also encourage the use of liberal praise and reinforcement when SW communicates appropriately and follows directions.

Reading

Given SW's considerable difficulties with language and reading, we recommend the school consider involving a reading specialist in his programming. Interventions should target faulty word recognition processes symptomatic of dyslexia by addressing deficits in phonological analysis/awareness. Sustained and systematic instruction should emphasize phonemic analysis (detection of sounds that comprise words), synthetic phonics (production of sounds that comprise letters and practice in blending), and reading fluency (additional practice in reading). Recent research has indicated that intervention needs to be between 30 and 60 minutes a day, 4 to 5 days a week, and delivered in a one-to-one, or, at most, a three-to-one, setting.

Information regarding reading programs that are based on empirical evidence for their effectiveness can be found in the *Report of the National Reading Panel* (http://www.nationalreadingpanel.org/Publications/publications.htm). Other helpful sources of information regarding reviews of reading interventions include the Institute of Education Sciences (http://ies.ed.gov/ncee/wwc/topic.aspx?sid=8), the Best Evidence Encyclopedia (http://www.bestevidence.org/reading/strug/top.htm), and the Florida Center for Reading Research (http://www.fcrr.org/interventions/Interventions.shtm). Several comprehensive reading programs that might also be considered are SRA Reading Mastery (http://www.mcgraw-hill.co.uk/sra/readingmastery.htm) and REACH (Reading Enriches All Children; http://reachreads.org/).

Please note that no single program—whether a comprehensive schoolwide program, reading technology, tutoring program, and so on—will be sufficient for all instructional reading needs. All reading programs, no matter how comprehensive, should be supported by other reading materials and initiatives. Although most programs described below are commercially available products, many teachers and students have created innovative and successful reading materials on their own. Not every method used to teach reading needs to be commercially prepared.

Recommendations for the Parents

ADHD and ODD

We strongly recommend parent behavioral management training using evidence-based programs for ADHD and disruptive behavior (ODD). For example, parent training programs by Barkley (2000—*Taking Charge of ADHD: The Complete, Authoritative Guide for Parents [Revised Edition]*; 1997—*Defiant Children: A Clinician's Manual for Assessment and Parent Training*), Kazdin (2008—*The Kazdin Method for Parenting the Defiant Child*), and Webster-Stratton (http://www.incredibleyears.com/) have excellent evidence for effectiveness.

We recommend considering another trial of medication for management of ADHD. Research shows that between 80% and 90% of children respond to medication with decreases in attentional difficulties and impulsivity. It is important for the effectiveness of medication to be informed by teacher report of SW's behavior within the school context. It is also important to note that there is no evidence to suggest that medication for ADHD will lead to substance abuse and dependence; in fact, substance abuse and dependence are likely to develop when ADHD and ODD are left untreated.

The best treatment for ADHD is the combination of parent behavioral management training and stimulant medication.

Anxiety

The evidence for treatment of school avoidance and anxiety is exposure to the feared situations (e.g., school). Therefore, we strongly recommend that SW not be permitted to avoid school or peer interactions, because this will only exacerbate symptoms further.

Individual Therapy

Individual therapy should now focus on parent behavioral management training so that SW and his family are receiving evidence-based treatment for ODD and ADHD, given that these issues are primarily contributing to his difficulties and impairment.

Coordination Across Providers, Parents, and Contexts

We recommend a joint meeting with all individuals involved in SW's care to develop a consistent approach to addressing these issues. A meeting could include us, the school, SW's mother and father, his psychotherapist, and pediatrician. SW will be best helped when there is consistency across contexts and individuals in his life.

It was a pleasure to work with SW. If there are any questions arising from this evaluation, please do not hesitate to contact our office at (111) 111-1111.

These results and recommendations were discussed during feedback sessions held with Ms. W on 09/19/2012 and Royal Coachman School District IEP team on 09/22/2012.

SUMMARY OF TEST RESULTS

HIGHLY CONFIDENTIAL: Please do not copy or distribute this information without specific permission.

Wechsler Abbreviated Scale of Intelligence—Second Edition

Scale	Standard Score	Percentile	Classification
Verbal Comprehension Index	76	5	Borderline
Perceptual Reasoning Index	100	50	Average
Full Scale IQ	87	19	Low average
Verbal subtests	Scaled score+	Percentile	
Vocabulary	6	9	
Similarities	5	5	
Performance subtests			
Block Design	10	50	
Matrix Reasoning	10	50	

Note. The Wechsler Abbreviated Scale of Intelligence—Second Edition provides an estimate/screening of cognitive functioning.

Wechsler Intelligence Scale For Children—Fourth Edition: Digit Span

Subtest	Scaled Score	Percentile
Digit Span	6	9

Note. Scaled Scores between 8 and 12 are considered to be average; scores below 7 are considered to be below average, and scores above 13 are considered to be above average.

Receptive One-Word Picture Vocabulary Test—Fourth Edition

Standard Score	Percentile	Age Equivalent
112	79	11-3[a]

Note. Scores between 89 and 110 are considered average, scores below 89 are considered below average, and scores above 110 are considered above average.
[a]11 years, 3 months.

FOLLOW-UP

The school district was very receptive to the feedback provided during the IEP meeting. The recommendations suggested by the psychologist were implemented into the IEP, and changes were made in SW's reading instruction. Ms. W, who was initially reluctant to restart stimulant medication, met again with pediatrician following the feedback session with psychologist. SW was restarted on medication. Because of the psychologist's work, the team of professionals working with SW all communicated with each other regarding his status. After several weeks of medication, the school psychologist reported a dramatic improvement in all academic areas, with particular improvement in handwriting legibility. In addition, SW was reported to be proud of his work and invested in doing well.

This case demonstrates the value of an IEE, the purpose of which is to provide information regarding a child's cognitive, academic, and psychological functioning. In this case, although the school and the parent were concerned about the student's behavior, a lack of communication between all of the professionals involved with the student interfered with the development of an effective intervention plan. More important, the psychologist who conducted the IEE was viewed by the parent as a neutral party who could be trusted and whose interest was solely on providing information to help the child. The psychologist's ability to discuss the findings of the evaluation, gather information from all of the professionals working with the child, and discuss empirically supported treatments was important in allaying the parent's concerns. This led to a positive outcome that would likely not have occurred had the IEE not been undertaken.

Appendix B
Independent Educational Evaluation: Parents' Agreement

This agreement addresses common issues that arise in independent educational evaluations. Please take the time to read through this document and review it with your attorney. If you have any questions, you can ask them in your initial meeting with me.

It is important that you understand in advance that this is an evaluation for legal purposes and that your child is my only client. There is a possibility that my impressions, conclusions, and recommendations may not be what you desire and may be unfavorable to your legal position. It is a very difficult and, at times, painful task to make recommendations that parents or caregivers may disagree with concerning a child's educational setting. However, this is my job, and that is why you are here.

The evaluation itself will consist of the psychological tests administered to your child; interviews with caregivers; and a review of relevant records, including school records, medical records, psychological assessments, and collateral interviews with third parties (e.g., other professionals involved with members of your family). This allows me to collect a wide range of data and organize the issues while minimizing the cost to you. (This statement would not be included in evaluations paid for by a school district.) During the interviews, you have the right to refuse to answer a question or line of questions. You also can ask to take a break from the interview, if necessary. At the end of the evaluation, a typed report with specific recommendations will be provided to you and the school district.

I recognize that my findings about your child's needs and impressions are very important to you; however, please do not ask me to give you an opinion until I have had an opportunity to hear all sides, review the psychological test results, and fully review the file of documents provided by all sources. We will schedule a time for me to discuss the results with you during a feedback session. A feedback session also will be scheduled with the school district.

Once the evaluation has begun, I cannot be a resource to you or anyone else involved in the case for advice, therapy, or support. These activities conflict with my role as a nonpartisan (i.e., neutral) evaluator.

You enter into this evaluation process by waiving confidentiality and releasing me from any and all liability for damages that might result from the release of information. You do so fully recognizing that my impressions, statements, reports, testimony, and other actions might be adverse and detrimental to you personally, financially, and to your legal position. I shall consider each child's interests ahead of any adult's interests. Anything discussed between any child and me shall remain confidential at my sole discretion, unless a court of law determines otherwise.

(The following two paragraphs do not apply to evaluations school districts pay for.)

You will pay a $_____ fee before the evaluation is begun. This is the charge for the evaluation up to discovery or courtroom testimony. It includes all face-to-face contact, phone calls, test scoring, and consultation with lawyers and other professionals involved with the case, as well as report preparation time. Your charges may be considerably higher than this amount if discovery and courtroom testimony occur. The reason the fee is paid up front reflects not on you but on the reality that I could not go into court with one party owing a large bill. This would leave me open to a question as to whether the financial situation had influenced my judgment. This is not an acceptable situation for you, and I will adhere strictly to this policy in order to avoid it.

The costs of providing an opportunity for your attorney to review the records, answering interrogatories, and providing testimony at a deposition or in court are often high and difficult to predict. I will charge an additional fee for reviewing records, responding to interrogatories, and/

or providing deposition or court testimony. Such a fee will include all travel, waiting, and professional service. The cost varies widely with the number and complexity of the issues, the number of children involved, and the degree of attorney and court involvement. An estimate of the time involved will be given to you, and payment is expected before I will engage in any of these additional services.

The policies and procedures described on this form were developed to help ensure that I am able to direct the evaluation toward recommendations that are in the best interests of the child or children involved. If after reviewing this information you have questions, please be sure to discuss them at your initial interview, when I will more fully explain the evaluation procedure you are about to begin.

This information and the procedures of an independent educational evaluation have been explained to me, and I agree to abide by these policies and have received a copy of this agreement.

DATE: _____ SIGNATURE OF PARTY: _____

I have reviewed this information with the party and the party agrees with the policies as evidenced by his/her signature.

DATE: _____ SIGNATURE OF EVALUATOR: _____

Appendix C
Summary of Independent Educational Evaluation for Parents

This is a description of the steps and the purposes of the procedures that are involved in the evaluation process. This evaluation will follow a structured pattern so as to maximize the fairness and the objectivity of the report and to work toward the best interests of your child. I will not discuss details or factors of the evaluation outside of the clinical interviews.

1. The first step of this process is for each side to agree to the evaluation. There must be a stipulated agreement or a court order that includes the following information:
   a. The precise nature and purpose of this appointment.
   b. An outline of the issues that are to be examined and addressed in the report. These issues need to be specific and framed in a manner so that they can be clearly addressed in the evaluation.
   c. A statement of who will pay for the evaluation.
   d. Permission to contact professionals and collaterals who have knowledge of the child.
   e. The expected due date or deadline for the completion and submission of the final report.

Evaluators: This document is intended to help parents understand the steps of the independent educational evaluation process.

Steps 2 through 4 are optional and depend on the psychologist's practice.

2. Payment for this evaluation must be made in advance. The first of two payments is required after the stipulated agreement is signed and before any other processing can take place. This first retainer fee covers the cost of the initial correspondence and the processing of a History Form and of a Disclosure Form.
3. Once the first retainer is paid, then the History Form and the Disclosure Form will be mailed to both parties.
4. The first clinical interview appointments will be scheduled after the History Form and the Disclosure Form are received back in my office.
5. The first clinical interview will require a least a 1.5-hour block of time. At this appointment, you should bring any written documents that you might think would be relevant.
6. I will begin the clinical interview by reviewing the Disclosure Form, asking and answering any questions you may have, and asking you to sign that document.
7. Next, you will be asked to complete standardized questionnaires that assess your child's social/emotional functioning, behavioral functioning, and adaptive behavior. The choice of questionnaires will depend on the referral questions and concerns raised in the interview.
8. After the structured interview, you will be asked to permit third party individuals who may be able to help with the evaluation to be contacted by me on your child's behalf.
9. You will also be asked to permit the release of relevant records, such as mental health records, medical records, school attendance and grade reports, achievement and standardized testing records, and psychological and educational testing reports.
10. The child will undergo psychological assessment. This will include tests of cognitive functioning, language, learning/memory, attention, academic skills, and problem solving. It may also include an interview with the child and measures of his or her psychological adjustment and emotional state. This may occur on the same day as the interview or on a subsequent day.

11. Once I have performed the assessment, consulted with third parties, and reviewed all the necessary documents, a feedback interview will be scheduled. This final interview will consist of two parts. First, I will attempt to clarify any details that are missing or that seem inconsistent with the findings of the evaluation. In the second part, you will be allowed the opportunity to examine how each of the findings was formed and to inquire about the details that led to the finding.
12. A meeting to discuss the findings and recommendations of the evaluation will be conducted with school officials.
13. You will be given a copy of the report, as will school officials.
14. If any further questions arise about the report, a conference call can be arranged, with both attorneys and school officials, if necessary.
15. If I am to serve as an expert witness during discovery or a due process hearing because the settlement process has failed, then an additional retainer will be required.

Appendix D
Common Mistakes to Avoid While Conducting Independent Educational Evaluations

We have seen many mistakes in evaluations we have reviewed while conducting our own independent educational evaluations. What follows is a nonexhaustive list of common mistakes that were mentioned in discussions with attorneys who specialize in special education law as well as ones we ourselves have seen. They all influence the reliability and validity of the evaluation. Worse, they may lead to inappropriate recommendations. We have also listed the possible impact of each error.

- Failing to ask if a student is on medications and whether he or she took medications on the day(s) of testing. IMPACT: Whether medications affected test performance is unknown, and it will be difficult to know whether the child's test performance represents his or her typical performance.
- Failing to review actual raw data regarding test protocols of prior evaluators. IMPACT: The evaluator may be unable to identify possible scoring errors in past evaluations, which may lead to wrong conclusions regarding changes in performance over time.
- Failing to record accurate dates of testing in relationship to external events or trauma. IMPACT: The evaluator may miss a potential relationship between the child's test performance and external events.
- Using outdated tests. IMPACT: Norms will be outdated; the evaluator may overestimate the child's performance due to the Flynn effect (the

gradual increase in intelligence test scores observed across the world in the past 75 years).

- Using standardized assessments without knowing their psychometric weakness. IMPACT: May lead to inaccurate conclusions regarding test performance, especially when comparing with other measures.
- Failure to reconcile contradictory information. IMPACT: The evaluator will be unable to support or refute clinical hypotheses.
- Citing a parent's or other evaluator's information as if one agrees with it. IMPACT: Confuses readers of the report regarding the evaluator's opinion.
- Failing to use measures that meet federal and state requirements for use in educational evaluations. IMPACT: Data cannot be used for eligibility determination.
- Describing average psychometric test results as *problems, deficits, impairments,* or *disabilities* on reports. IMPACT: Such an inaccurate description of a child's performance suggests that he or she has deficits or weaknesses when in fact none are present.
- Failing to consider the meaningfulness of test scores (e.g., failure to consider the concept of the standard error of measurement). IMPACT: May lead to either over- or underestimation of the child's performance.
- Transcription or scoring mistakes. IMPACT: Invalid scores may be interpreted and presumed valid.
- Describing a static condition as "delayed" development. IMPACT: May misrepresent the child's potential for progress.
- Failing to consult with school staff before writing the report. IMPACT: The validity of the findings, as well as the recommendations, may be significantly compromised.
- Failing to assess possible bias, self-interest, or conflicts of the person providing diagnostically relevant medical or other background history. IMPACT: The validity of the report may be compromised.
- Failing to review all medical records to verify parent/school history. IMPACT: Impressions and recommendations may be inaccurate.
- Failing to actually talk with previous service providers or evaluators. IMPACT: Impressions and recommendations may be inaccurate.

- Teachers not filling out checklists candidly. IMPACT: Impressions and recommendations may be inaccurate.
- Misunderstanding congressional definitions included in statutes. IMPACT: Conclusions regarding qualification eligibility may be inaccurate.

In addition to the preceding items, evaluators should consider the following questions, and the potential impact of the answers, before completing a report:

- Was prior testing done in summer, in early September, the day before or after winter break, or at other times that might lead to lower scores or low test motivation? IMPACT: Reliability of scores may be reduced.
- Was testing done all in one session or across many sessions? IMPACT: Consider the child's typical performance: Spending multiple 1-hour sessions on testing may not reflect the way the test's norms were collected.
- Did the evaluator use methods that involve rigorous data analyses that are adequate to test the stated hypotheses and justify the conclusions drawn? IMPACT: If not, the reliability and validity of data, as well as the evaluator's overall impressions, could be compromised.

References

Achenbach, T. M., & Rescorla, R. A. (2001). *Manual for the ASEBA School-Age Forms and Profiles.* Burlington: University of Vermont, Research Center for Children, Youth, and Families.

Ackerman, M. J. (2006). Forensic report writing. *Journal of Clinical Psychology, 62,* 59–72. doi:10.1002/jclp.20200

American Academy of Clinical Neuropsychology. (2007). American Academy of Clinical Neuropsychology (AACN) practice guidelines for neuropsychological assessment and consultation. *The Clinical Neuropsychologist, 21,* 209–231. doi:10.1080/13825580601025932

American Psychiatric Association. (1987). *Diagnostic and statistical manual of mental disorders* (3rd ed., revised). Washington, DC: Author.

American Psychiatric Association. (1994). *Diagnostic and statistical manual of mental disorders* (4th ed.). Washington, DC: Author.

American Psychological Association. (2002). Ethical principles of psychologists and code of conduct. Retrieved from *American Psychologist, 57,* 1060–1073.

American Psychological Association. (2005). APA 2020: A perfect vision for psychology: 2004 five-year report of the policy and planning board. *American Psychologist, 60,* 512–522. doi:10.1037/0003-066X.60.5.512

American Psychological Association. (2010). 2010 amendments to the 2002 "Ethical Principles of Psychologists and Code of Conduct." *American Psychologist, 65,* 493.

American Psychological Association. (2012). *Appropriate use of high-stakes testing in our nation's schools.* Retrieved from http://www.apa.org/pubs/info/brochures/testing.aspx

American Psychological Association Council of Representatives. (2008). *Approved minutes, August 13 and 17, 2008.* Retrieved from http://www.apa.org/about/governance/council/08aug-crminutes.aspx

Americans With Disabilities Act of 1990, 42 U.S.C. § 12101 *et seq.*

Aud, S., Hussar, W., Kena, G., Bianco, K., Frohlich, L., Kemp, J., & Tahan, K. (2011). *The condition of education 2011* (Publication NCES 2011-033). Washington, DC: National Center for Education Statistics.

Barkley, R. A. (1997). *Defiant children: A clinician's manual for assessment and parent training* (2nd ed.). New York, NY: Guilford Press.

Barkley, R. A. (2000). *Taking charge of ADHD: The complete, authoritative guide for parents* (revised ed.). New York, NY: Guilford Press.

Barkley, R. A. (2012). *Barkley Deficits in Executive Functioning Scale—Children and Adolescents.* New York, NY: Guilford Press.

Baron, I. S. (2004). *Neuropsychological evaluation of the child.* Oxford, England: Oxford University Press.

Benjamin, A. G., & Gollan, J. K. (2003). *Family evaluation in custody litigation: Reducing risks of ethical infractions and malpractice.* Washington, DC: American Psychological Association.

Bennett, B. E., Bryant, B. K., VandenBos, G. R., & Greenwood, A. (1990). *Professional liability and risk management.* Washington, DC: American Psychological Association. doi:10.1037/11102-000

Boyle, C. A., Boulet, S., Schieve, L. A., Cohen, R. A., Blumberg, S. J., Yeargin-Allsopp, M., . . . Kogan, M. D. (2011). Trends in the prevalence of developmental disabilities in US children, 1997–2008. *Pediatrics, 127,* 1034–1042. doi:10.1542/peds.2010-2989

Brenner, E. (2003). Consumer-focused psychological assessment. *Professional Psychology: Research and Practice, 34,* 240–247. doi:10.1037/0735-7028.34.3.240

Brodsky, S. L. (2012). *Testifying in court: Guidelines and maxims for expert witnesses* (2nd ed.). Washington, DC: American Psychological Association.

Brooks, B. L., & Iverson, G. L. (2012). Improving accuracy when identifying cognitive impairment in pediatric neuropsychological assessments. In E. M. S. Sherman & B. L. Brooks (Eds.), *Pediatric forensic neuropsychology* (pp. 66–88). New York, NY: Oxford University Press.

Centers for Disease Control and Prevention. (2008). Prevalence of autism spectrum disorders—Autism and Developmental Disabilities Monitoring Network, 14 sites, United States, 2008. *Surveillance Summaries, 61*(3), 1–19.

Cleary, M. J., & Scott, A. J. (2011). Developments in clinical neuropsychology: Implications for school psychological services. *Journal of School Health, 81,* 1–7. doi:10.1111/j.1746-1561.2010.00550.x

Definitions, 34 C.F.R. § 104.3 (2010).

Designation of Responsible Employee and Adoption of Grievance Procedures, 34 C. F. R. § 104.7 (2010).

Development, Review, and Revision of IEP, 34 C.F.R. § 300.324 (2010).

Educational Setting, 34 C.F.R. 104.34 (2010).

Elementary and Secondary Education Act of 1965, 20 U.S.C. ch. 70.

Ernst, W. J., Pelletier, S. L. F., & Simpson, G. (2008). Neuropsychological consultation with school personnel: What clinical neuropsychologists need to know. *The Clinical Neuropsychologist, 22*, 953–976. doi:10.1080/138540407 01676591

Evaluation and Placement, 34 C.F.R. § 104.35 (2010).

Fogt, J. B., Miller, D. N., & Zirkel, P. A. (2003). Defining autism: Professional best practices and published case law. *Journal of School Psychology, 41*, 201–216. doi:10.1016/S0022-4405(03)00045-1

Fombonne, E. (2005). The changing epidemiology of autism. *Journal of Applied Research in Intellectual Disabilities, 18*, 281–294. doi:10.1111/j.1468-3148.2005. 00266.x

Frick, P. J., Barry, C. T., & Kamphaus, R. W. (2010). *Clinical assessment of child and adolescent personality and behavior* (3rd ed.). New York, NY: Springer. doi:10.1007/978-1-4419-0641-0

Garb, H. N. (1989). Clinical judgment, clinical training, and professional experience. *Psychological Bulletin, 105*, 387–396. doi:10.1037/0033-2909.105.3.387

Garb, H. N. (2005). Clinical judgment and decision making. *Annual Review of Clinical Psychology, 1*, 67–89. doi:10.1146/annurev.clinpsy.1.102803.143810

Gioia, G., Isquith, P. K., Guy, S. C., & Kenworthy, L. (2003). *Behavior Rating Inventory of Executive Function.* San Antonio, TX: The Psychological Corporation.

Harvey, V. S. (2006). Variables affecting the clarity of psychological reports. *Journal of Clinical Psychology, 62*, 5–18. doi:10.1002/jclp.20196

Hurewitz, F., & Kerr, S. (2011). The role of the independent neuropsychologist in special education. *The Clinical Neuropsychologist, 25*, 1058–1074.

IEP Team, 34 C.F.R. § 300.321 (2010).

Independent Educational Evaluation, 34 C.F.R. § 300.502 (2010).

Individuals With Disabilities Education Improvement Act of 2004, 20 U.S.C. § 1400 *et seq.*

Kahneman, D. (2011). *Thinking, fast and slow.* New York, NY: Farrar, Straus and Giroux.

Kanne, S. M., Randolph, J., & Farmer, J. (2008). Diagnostic and assessment findings: A bridge to academic planning for children with autism spectrum disorders. *Neuropsychology Review, 18*, 367–384. doi:10.1007/s11065-008-9072-z

Kazdin, A. (2008). *The Kazdin method for parenting the defiant child.* New York, NY: Mariner Books.

Kerr, D. C. R., Lunkenheimer, E. S., & Olson, S. L. (2007). Assessment of child problem behaviors by multiple informants: A longitudinal study from preschool to school entry. *Journal of Child Psychology and Psychiatry, 48,* 967–975. doi:10.1111/j.1469-7610.2007.01776.x

Kirkwood, M. W. (2012). Overview of tests and techniques to detect negative response bias in children. In E. M. S. Sherman & B. L. Brooks (Eds.), *Pediatric forensic neuropsychology* (pp. 136–161). New York, NY: Oxford University Press.

Kirkwood, M. W., Yeates, K. O., Randolph, C., & Kirk, J. W. (2012). The implications of symptom validity test failure for ability-based test performance in a pediatric sample. *Psychological Assessment, 24,* 36–45. doi:10.1037/a0024628

Kovacs, M. (2011). *Children's Depression Inventory 2.* North Tonawanda, NY: Multi-Health Systems.

Lai, S. A., & Berkeley, S. (2012). High-stakes test accommodations: Research and practice. *Learning Disability Quarterly, 35,* 158–169.

Luke, S. D., & Schwartz, A. (2007). Assessment and accommodations. *Evidence for Education, 2*(1), 1–8. Retrieved from http://nichcy.org/wp-content/uploads/docs/eeaccommodations.pdf

Luvera, P. N. (1981). *The efficient law office.* Seattle, WA: Butterworth.

MacFarlane, J. R., & Kanaya, T. (2009). What does it mean to be autistic? Interstate variation in special education criteria for autism services. *Journal of Child and Family Studies, 18,* 662–669. doi:10.1007/s10826-009-9268-8

Madaus, J. W., & Shaw, S. F. (2007). The role of school professionals in implementing section 504 for students with disabilities. *Educational Policy, 22,* 363–378. doi:10.1177/0895904807307069

Mastoras, S. M., Climie, E. A., McCrimmon, A. W., & Schwean, V. L. (2011). A C.L.E.A.R. approach to report writing: A framework for improving the efficacy of psychoeducational reports. *Canadian Journal of School Psychology, 26,* 127–147. doi:10.1177/0829573511409722

McBride, G., Dumont, R., & Willis, J. O. (2011). *Essentials of IDEA for assessment professionals.* Hoboken, NJ: Wiley.

Merikangas, K. R., He, J. P., Brody, D., Fisher, P. W., Bourdon, K., & Koretz, D. S. (2010). Prevalence and treatment of mental disorders among US children in the 2001–2004 NHANES. *Pediatrics, 125,* 75–81. doi:10.1542/peds.2008-2598

Michaels, M. H. (2006). Ethical considerations in writing psychological assessment reports. *Journal of Clinical Psychology, 62,* 47–58. doi:10.1002/jclp.20199

National Association of School Psychologists. (2009). *Recruitment of culturally and linguistically diverse school psychologists.* Bethesda, MD: Author.

National Education Association. (2012). *Impact of sequestration on federal education programs.* Retrieved from http://educationvotes.nea.org/wp-content/uploads/2012/10/09-14-12SequestrationAll.pdf

New America Foundation. (2012). *Individuals With Disabilities Education Act: Cost impact on local school districts.* Retrieved from http://febp.newamerica. net/background-analysis/individuals-disabilities-education-act-cost-impact- local-school-districts

Nichols, S. L. (2007). High-stakes testing: Does it increase achievement? *Journal of Applied School Psychology, 23,* 47–64. doi:10.1300/J370v23n02_04

No Child Left Behind Act of 2001, Pub. L. No. 107-110, 115 Stat. 1425 (2002).

Nonacademic Services, 34 C.F.R. § 104.37 (2010).

Nondiscrimination on the Basis of Handicap in Programs or Activities Receiving Federal Financial Assistance, 34 C. F. R. § 104 (2010).

Pappas, E. H. (1987). Preparing your witness for deposition. *For the Defense, 29,* 8–9.

Patient Protection and Affordable Care Act, Pub. L. No. 111-148, 124 Stat. 119 (2010).

Pope, K. S. (1992). Responsibilities in providing psychological test feedback to clients. *Psychological Assessment, 4,* 268–271. doi:10.1037/1040-3590.4.3.268

Procedural Safeguards, 34 C.F.R. 104.36 (2010).

Rehabilitation Act of 1973, 29 U.S.C. § 701 *et seq.*

Reynolds, C. R., & Horton, A. M., Jr., (Eds.). (2012). *Detection of malingering during head injury litigation.* New York, NY: Springer. doi:10.1007/978-1-4614-0442-2

Reynolds, C. R., & Kamphaus, R. W. (2004). *Behavioral Assessment System for Children—Second edition.* San Antonio, TX: The Psychological Corporation.

Roberts, R. E., Roberts, C. R., & Xing, Y. (2007). Rates of *DSM–IV* psychiatric disorders among adolescents in a large metropolitan area. *Journal of Psychiatric Research, 41,* 959–967. doi:10.1016/j.jpsychires.2006.09.006

Sattler, J. M. (2008). *Assessment of children: Cognitive foundations* (5th ed.). San Diego, CA: Author.

Sattler, J. M., & Hoge, R. D. (2006). *Assessment of children: Behavioral, social, and clinical foundations* (5th ed.). San Diego, CA: Jerome M. Sattler.

Schaffer v. Weast, 546 U.S. 49 (2005).

Schrank, F. A., Miller, J. A., Caterino, L. C., & Desrochers, J. (2006). American Academy of School Psychology survey on the independent educational evaluation for a specific learning disability: Results and discussion. *Psychology in the Schools, 43,* 771–780. doi:10.1002/pits.20187

Schraven, J., & Jolly, J. L. (2010). Section 504 in American public schools: An ongoing response to change. *American Educational Historical Journal, 37,* 419–436.

Scull, J., & Winkler, A. M. (2011). *Shifting trends in special education.* Washington, DC: Thomas B. Fordham Institute.

Shaffer, D., Fisher, P., Dulcan, M. K., Davies, M., Piacentini, J., Schwab-Stone, M. E., . . . Regier, D. A. (1996). The NIMH Diagnostic Interview Schedule for Children Version 2.3 (DISC-2.3): Description, acceptability, prevalence rates, and performance in the MECA Study. *Journal of the American Academy of Child & Adolescent Psychiatry, 35,* 865–877. doi:10.1097/00004583-199607000-00012

Sherman, E. M. S., & Brooks, B. L. (2012). *Pediatric forensic neuropsychology.* New York, NY: Oxford University Press

Supovitz, J. (2009). Can high stakes testing leverage educational improvement? Prospects from the last decade of testing and accountability reform. *Journal of Educational Change, 10,* 211–227. doi:10.1007/s10833-009-9105-2

TeamChild. (2008). *Make a difference in a child's life: A manual for helping children and youth get what they need in school.* Retrieved from http://www.dshs.wa.gov/pdf/ca/TeamChildMannual.pdf

Tombaugh, T. N. (1996). *Test of Memory Malingering.* San Antonio, TX: The Psychological Corporation.

Watson, A. S. (1978). On the preparation and use of psychiatric expert testimony: Some suggestions in the ongoing controversy. *Bulletin of the American Academy of Psychiatry and the Law, 6,* 226–246.

Wechsler, D. (1991). *Wechsler Intelligence Scale for Children—Third edition.* San Antonio, TX: The Psychological Corporation.

Wechsler, D. (2004). *Wechsler Intelligence Scale for Children—Fourth edition.* London, England: Pearson Assessments.

Wilkinson, L. A. (2010). *A best practice guide to assessment and intervention for autism and Asperger syndrome in schools.* London, England: Kingsley.

World Health Organization. (2010). *International statistical classification of diseases and related health problems, 10th revision.* Geneva, Switzerland: Author.

Ysseldyke, J., Nelson, J. R., Christenson, S., Johnson, D. R., Dennison, A., Triezenberg, H., . . . Hawes, M. (2004). What we know and need to know about the consequences of high-stakes testing for students with disabilities. *Exceptional Children, 71,* 75–94.

Index

Accommodations, for high-stakes
testing, 18
Administrative law judge, 31
Administrative proceedings, for IEP
disputes, 31–33
Adolescents, and feedback session, 67
Age equivalents, 69
American Academy of Clinical
Neuropsychology, 64
ASD. *See* Autism spectrum disorders
Assessment procedures, 78
Assessment tools
approval of, by states, 55
federal/state requirements for, 124
knowing weaknesses of, 124
in psychological reports, 78
Attorneys
for due process hearings, 31–32
in due process trials, 84
intent of, 83
involvement of, in evaluations,
40, 41
Autism and Developmental Disabilities
Monitoring Network, 9
Autism spectrum disorders (ASD)
DSM vs. IDEIA in evaluations of
children with, 15
not included in prevalence rates, 8–9

variability in legal code impacting
children with, 22

Background, of child, 77–78
BASC 2, 53
Behavioral functioning, 51–52
Behavior observations
during feedback sessions, 68
in psychological reports, 78
Broadband behavior checklists, 52

Case example
conducting IEEs in, 60–62
feedback in, 72
Child find (term), 11
Childhood onset disorders, 52
Children
age birth to 3 years, 33–35
background of, in reports, 77–78
with disabilities, legal rights
of, 21
explaining psychological testing to,
53–54
history of, in reports, 77–78
importance of education
experience for, 4–5
participation in feedback session
by, 66–67

Clinical framework, for evaluations, 14–17
Clinical interviews, 45
Conditions, diagnosable, 16–17
Conducting IEEs, 39–62
    accepting referrals, 42–45
    administering parent questionnaires, 53
    administering psychological testing with child, 53–56
    administering semistructured interview, 49–52
    in case example, 60–62
    completing release-of-information forms, 52–53
    and disclosure process, 46–48
    immediate review of data from, 57–59
    interviewing teachers and school personnel, 56–57
    mistakes while, 123–125
    obtaining records for review, 57
    preparing for first clinical interviews, 45
    preparing release-of-information forms, 45–46
    process of, explaining to family, 48–49
    referrals for, 39–42
    when requested by school district, 59–60
Confidentiality statement, 76
Consent
    of parents, for early intervention services, 34
    of parents, for evaluations, 24
    of parents, for special education services, 28
Contradictory information, 124
Credibility, of evaluators, 87–89
Cross-examination, 88–90
Curriculum-based measures, 22
Custody evaluations, 59

Data, immediate review of, 57–59
Data collection, 22
Developmental disabilities, 9
Developmental factors, 50–51
Developmental history, 77
Diagnosable conditions, 16–17
Diagnoses, in psychological reports, 79
Diagnostic and Statistical Manual of Mental Disorders (DSM), 8, 15. See also specific editions
Direct examination, 86–88
Disabilities
    defined under Section 504, 35
    determined by eligibility-determination group, 25
Disclosure agreement, 48
Disclosure process, 16, 46–48
Dispute-resolution procedures, 36–37
Domains
    of assessment, and IDEIA, 54
    significant findings discussed by, 78–79
DSM (Diagnostic and Statistical Manual of Mental Disorders), 8, 15. See also specific editions
DSM–5, 8n
DSM–III–R, 8
DSM–IV, 8
Due process hearings, 83–91
    acting as expert witness during, 85–90
    and postruling interactions, 90–91
    process of, 84–85
    to resolve IEP-related disputes, 31–33

Early Intervention Program, 21
Early intervention services, 33–35
Educational framework, for evaluations, 14–17

Educational laws, 21–37
    for children age birth to 3 years,
        33–35
    and IEP-related dispute resolution,
        30–33
    legal process for evaluation under,
        24–30
    requests for evaluation under,
        23–24
    Section 504 of Rehabilitation Act
        of 1973, 35–37
    state vs. federal, 21–22
    understanding definitions in, 125
    and usefulness of evaluations,
        22–23
Educational professionals, 22
Eligibility-determination group, 25–26
Emotional functioning, 51–52
Environmental stressors, 16–17
Ernst, W. J., 10, 23, 43
Errors, in conducting IEEs, 123–125
Ethical Principles of Psychologists and
    Code of Conduct (APA), 63
Ethical standards, for psychologists, 23
Evaluations
    custody, 59
    for early intervention services, 33
    lacking schools' interaction, 12
    legal process for, 24–30
    purposes of, 14
    requests for, 23–24
    required by Section 504, 36
    usefulness of, 22–23
Evaluators
    behavior of, in due process
        hearings, 84
    credibility of, 87–89
    as expert witnesses, 85–90
    and familiarity with state
        criteria, 56
    impressions of, in reports, 79–80
    role of, 48–49
Expert witnesses, 85–90

Families
    explaining IEE process to, 48–49
    and feedback sessions, 64–65
    input on recommendations by, 71
Family service coordinators, 35
Federal educational laws, 21–22
Feedback, 63–73
    in case example, 72
    defined, 63
    and IEP meetings, 72–73
    options for providing, 64–65
    process of providing, 66–72
Feedback sessions
    drafted version of clinical
        interview used in, 57–58
    importance of, 63–64
    scheduling, 49
Financial penalties, for schools, 35–36
Findings, significant, 78–79
Flynn effect, 123–124

Grade equivalents, 69

Hearing officers, 29–31
High-stakes testing, 17–18
History
    of child, in psychological report,
        77–78
    of child, properly reviewed for
        evaluation, 124
    developmental, 77
    medical, 77
    school, 77–78
    social, 77
Hurewitz, F., 79–80

ICD-10 (International Statistical
    Classification of Diseases and
    Related Health Problems), 8n
IDEIA
    as basis for IEEs, 15–16
    children eligible for services
        under, 7

disabilities under, 11
and domains of assessment, 54
and high-stakes testing, 18
mediation under, 30–31
and members of IEP teams, 27
and requests for evaluation, 23–24
and research-based interventions, 80
schools required to consider IEEs
    under, 43
Section 504 vs., 13, 35–36
used for diagnoses, 54–55
used for evaluations, 15
IEEs
IEPs vs., 70
legal rights of parents to obtain, 12
right of parents to, 29–30
IEP meetings, 72–73
IEPs
appropriateness of, 84
as guide for special education
    services, 13
IEEs vs., 70
implementation of, 28
mandatory contents of, 27–28
resolution of disputes over, 30–33
revision of, 28–29
timeframe for designing, 26
IEP teams, 26–27, 80
IFSPs (individualized family service
    plans), 33–35
IHO (Impartial Hearing Officer), 84
Impartial Hearing Officer (IHO), 84
Impressions (of evaluators), 79–80
Inconsistent testimony, 89
Independent clinical psychologists,
    14–15
Independent Educational Evaluation:
    Parents' Agreement (sample),
    115–117
Independent educational evaluation
    report (sample), 95–113
Independent educational evaluations.
    See IEEs

Individualized education plans.
    See IEPs
Individualized family service plans
    (IFSPs), 33–35
Individuals With Disabilities
    Education Improvement Act of
    2004. See IDEIA
Information
contradictory, 124
identifying, in psychological
    reports, 76
not relevant to IEE, in feedback
    sessions, 64, 65
from others, 124
personal, 16–17
personal, revealed in IEEs, 16–17
referral, in psychological reports,
    76
shared in feedback sessions, 49
Informed consent form, 47
International Statistical Classification
    of Diseases and Related Health
    Problems (ICD-10), 8n
Interventions, research-based, 80
Interviews
clinical, 45
semistructured, 49–52
of teachers and school personnel,
    56–57

Jolly, J. L., 35–36

Kanaya, T., 22
Kerr, S., 79–80

Language
and readability of reports, 68–69
use of, in evaluations, 124
use of, in testimony, 88
Leading questions, 89–90
Legal process, for evaluations, 24–30
Legal professionals, 22

Legal rights, of children with
disabilities, 21
Legal standards, for evaluations,
10–11
Litigation process, 84

MacFarlane, J. R., 22
Madaus, J., 26
Mediation, for IEP disputes, 30–31
Medical disorders, 55
Medical history, 77
Medication, 123
Methodology, of evaluations, 29
Methodology for Epidemiology of
Mental Disorders in Children
and Adolescents study, 8

National Association of School
Psychologists, 10
National Center for Education
Statistics, 7
No Child Left Behind Act of 2001
(NCLB), 17

Opinions, supporting, 88
Outdated tests, 123–124

Parent-initiated referrals, 39–42
Parent questionnaires, 53
Parents
concerns of, discussed during
clinical interviews, 50
consent of, for early intervention
services, 34
consent of, for evaluations, 24
consent of, for special education
services, 28
and educational experience, 5
evaluations initiated by, 11–12
requests for evaluation by, 23–24
Parents' Agreement, in IEE (sample),
115–117
Parsimonious testimony, 88

PDDs (pervasive developmental
disorders), 8–9
Pelletier, S. L. F., 10, 23
Personal information, 16–17
Pervasive developmental disorders
(PDDs), 8–9
Pope, K. S., 63
Postruling interactions, 90–91
Postschool activities, 28
Psychological reports, 75–82
assessment tools/procedures in, 78
behavior observations in, 78
child's background/history in,
77–78
impressions (of evaluators) in,
79–80
recommendations in, 80–81
score summary in, 81
significant findings in, 78–79
Psychological testing, 53–56
Psychologists
collaboration of, with schools, 71
data collection by, 22
identification of special needs
children by, 3
independent clinical vs. school,
14–15
participation in IEP meetings by,
72–73

Qualification, of evaluators, 85–86

Recommendations
academic relevance of, 49–50
discussed in feedback sessions,
69–72
in psychological reports, 80–81
Records
access to, denied by parents, 43–44
obtaining, for review, 57
potentially informative, 53
Redirect examination, 90
Reevaluations, 29, 36

Referrals
accepting, 42–45
for IEEs, 39–42
parent-initiated, 39–42
Rehabilitation Act of 1973, 35. *See also* Section 504
Release-of-information forms, 45–46, 52–53
Reports, psychological. *See* Psychological reports
Requests for evaluation, 23–24
Research-based interventions, 80
Resolution session, 32
Results, of assessments, 68
Review
annual, of IEPs, 28
of evaluation reports, before due process hearings, 85
of IFSPs, 34
immediate, of data for IEEs, 57–59
of records, before evaluation, 44, 45
of records, for IEEs, 57

Sattler, J. M., 69
School history, 77–78
School personnel, 56–57
School psychologists, 14–15
Schools
collaboration of, with psychologists, 71
consulting with, for evaluations, 124
decline of requests for evaluation by, 29–30
and feedback sessions, 64–65
IEEs requested by, 59–60
input for recommendations by, 71
lack of interaction with evaluator by, 12
Schraven, J., 35–36
Section 504 (of Rehabilitation Act of 1973)

content of evaluations governed by, 12–13
disabilities under, 10–11
educational laws, 35–37
IDEIA vs., 13, 35–36
and requests for evaluation, 23–24
used for evaluations, 15
Section 504 compliance officer, 25
Section 504 plans, 36
Seeking Consultation (term), 40–41
Seeking Help (term), 40
Seeking Resolution (term), 41
Semistructured interview, 49–52
Shaw, S., 26
Significant findings, 78–79
Simpson, G., 10, 23
Social functioning, 51–52
Social history, 77
Special education evaluations, 7–19
clinical vs. educational framework for, 14–17
context of, 7–10
and high-stakes testing, 17–18
legal standards for, 10–11
and special education services, 12–13
types of, 11–12
Special education funding, 9
Special education services
consent of parents for, 28
IEPs as guide for, 13
percentage of children receiving, 7
and special education evaluations, 12–13
Standard 9.01, Bases for Assessments (APA), 44
State educational laws, 21–22
Stressors, environmental, 16–17
Summary of Independent Educational Evaluation for Parents (sample), 119–121
Symptom validity measure, 54

Teachers
information provided by, 125
interviewing, for IEEs, 56–57
Testimony
of evaluators in due process
hearings, 85–90
inconsistent, 89
parsimonious, 88
Testing
considering previous, 125
high-stakes, 17–18
psychological, 53–56

Test of Memory Malingering, 54
Tests, outdated, 123–124
Test scores
discussed in feedback sessions,
68–69
in evaluations, 123, 124
summaries of, in reports, 81
Timelines, for evaluations, 24

Voir dire, 86

Wilkinson, L. A., 15
Witnesses, expert, 85–90

About the Authors

David Breiger, PhD, received his doctorate in developmental and clinical neuropsychology from the University of Houston in 1986. He is a clinical associate professor in the Department of Psychiatry and Behavioral Sciences and the Department of Psychology at the University of Washington, Seattle and the director of the Neuropsychological Consultation Service at Seattle Children's Hospital.

His clinical interests for the past 26 years have been the neuropsychological assessment of children and helping children adjust to neurodevelopmental and neurocognitive challenges. He supervises psychology postdoctoral fellows, psychology residents, and psychology graduate students. He teaches the Intellectual Assessment graduate courses in the University of Washington's Department of Psychology. Dr. Breiger was awarded the Outstanding Supervisor award from the University of Washington of Psychology Internship Program.

His research is currently focused on the relationship between brain development and neuropsychological functioning in children who have been treated for brain tumors. He has coauthored a number of articles and book chapters.

Kristen Bishop, PsyD, is a recent graduate entering the field of clinical psychology. Her dissertation, "Creating Academic Recommendations for Children With an Autism Spectrum Disorder: Insights From Key

Informants," explored how psychologists could improve their academic recommendations for children with an autism spectrum disorder.

Her professional interests include academic child assessment, collaborative work with school-based professionals, and conducting assessments and providing treatments for children with neurodevelopmental disabilities. Her interest in providing interdisciplinary assessment that best supports a child's treatment across settings including the home, school, and community can be seen in her clinical training and experience. Dr. Bishop's training and experience include the completion of the Parenting Evaluation Training Program at the University of Washington and the University of Washington's Leadership Education in Neurodevelopmental and Related Disabilities long-term trainee certificate. She will soon be beginning private practice work, including assessment and treatment services, through Eastside Psychological Associates in Washington State.

G. Andrew H. Benjamin, JD, PhD, ABPP, is the director of the Parenting Evaluation/Training Program at the University of Washington in Seattle as well as clinical professor of psychology and affiliate professor of law at the University of Washington. While working with families engaged in high-conflict litigation and lawyers suffering from various mental health and drug abuse problems, Dr. Benjamin was named "Professional of the Year" by the Washington State Bar Association's Family Law Section. He was elected to serve as president of the Washington State Psychological Association, and later his colleagues there created an association award named after him for "outstanding and tireless contributions." He was honored by the Puyallup Indian Nation's Health Authority for serving as a "modern day warrior fighting the mental illnesses, drug-alcohol addictions" of the people served by the Nation's program. After being elected representative of Washington to the American Psychological Association's (APA's) Council of Representatives for two terms, Dr. Benjamin was appointed the council's parliamentarian and served in that capacity for four terms. He has served as a member and a chair of APA's Committee on Legal Issues and APA's Policy and Planning Board. He is the past president of APA's Division for States, Provinces and Territories and a member of the APA Board of Educational Affairs. APA conferred on him the Heiser Award in recognition of his record of public service and advocacy in numerous areas of professional activity.

Dr. Benjamin has published 59 peer-reviewed articles in psychology, law, and psychiatry journals. He is the coauthor of three books published by APA—*Law and Mental Health Professionals; Family Evaluation in Custody Litigation: Reducing Risks of Ethical Infractions and Malpractice;* and *The Duty to Protect: Ethical, Legal, and Professional Considerations for Mental Health Professionals*—and one book published by Sage: *Ethics for Psychologists: A Casebook Approach.* Two of his lectures about issues related to child custody are posted online at http://www.youtube.com/user/TheFoundation1020?feature=mhee.